2005

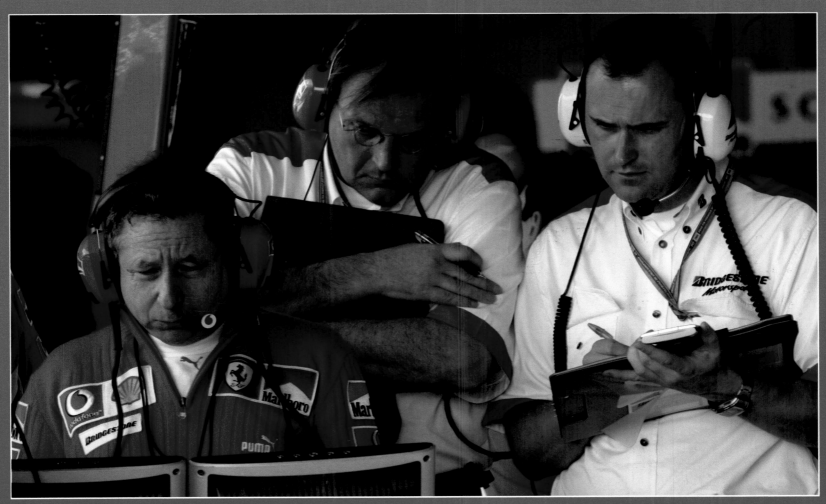

CREDIT SUISSE
PETRONAS MALAYSIA
MICHELIN
MAGNETI MARELLI
SAUBER
CERTINA
1888
DS PODIUM
TACHYMETER

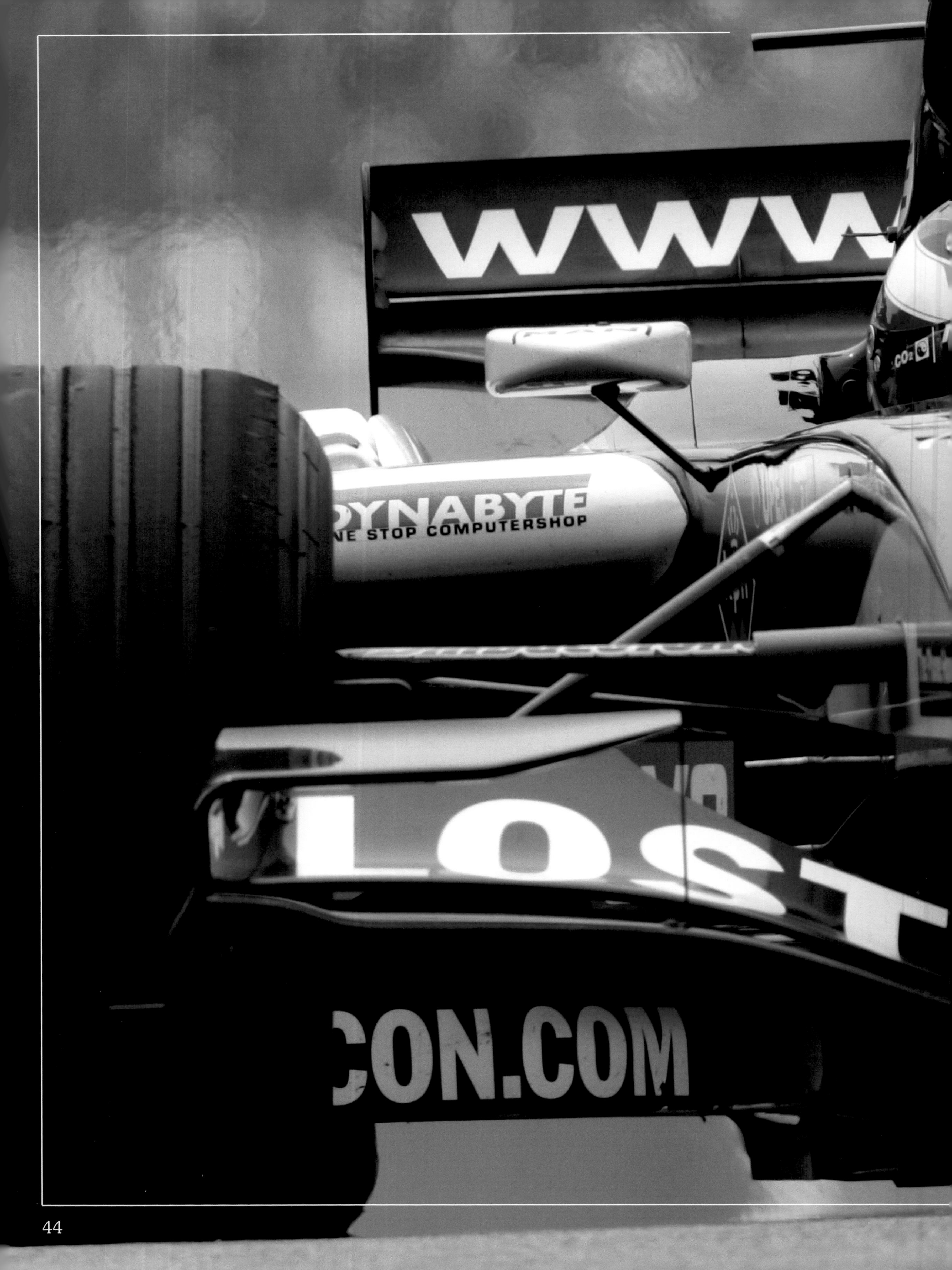
WWW
DYNABYTE
NE STOP COMPUTERSHOP
LOST
CON.COM

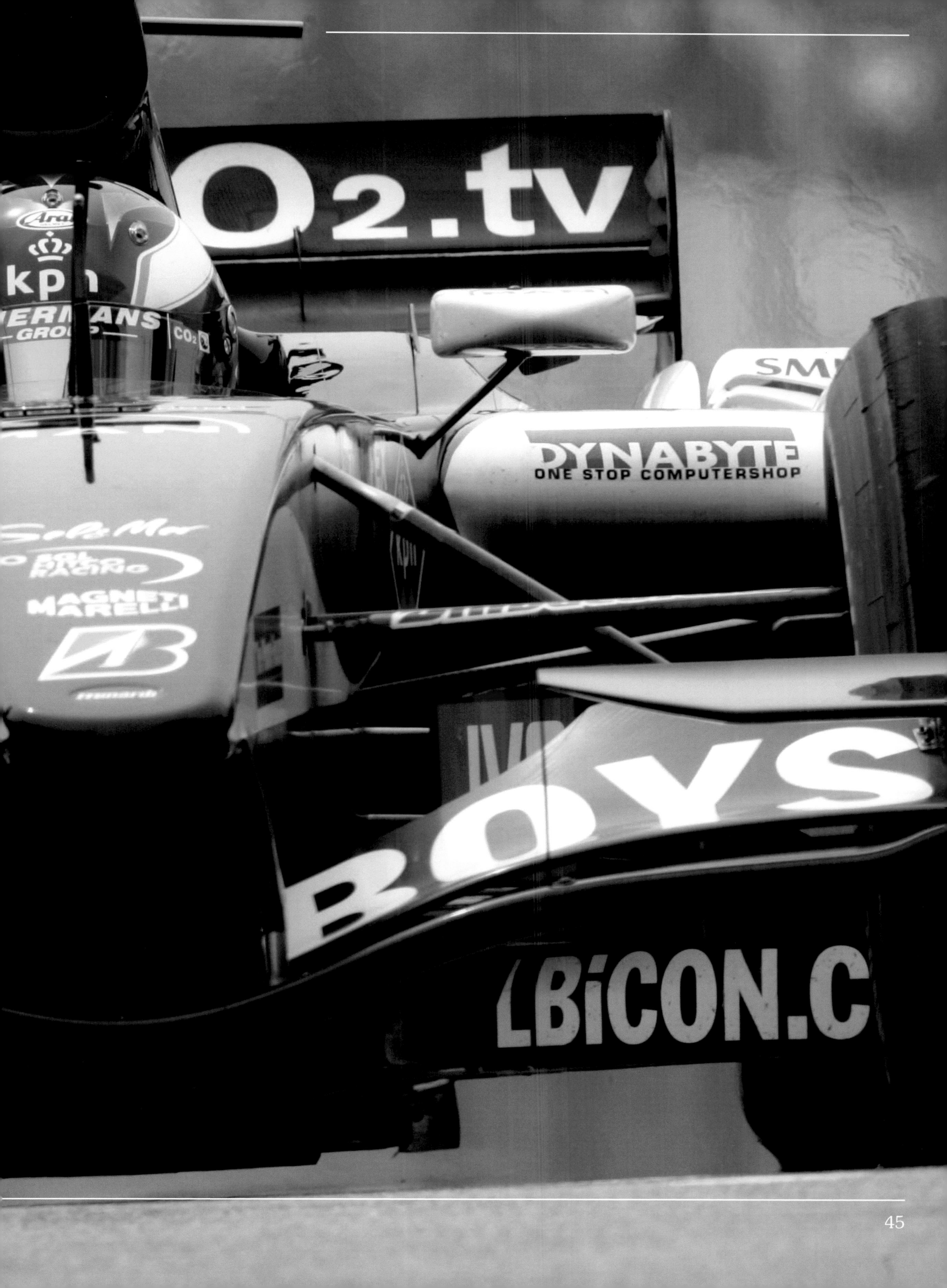
O2.tv
kpn
DYNABYTE
ONE STOP COMPUTERSHOP
MAGNETI MARELLI

HOW THE MIGHTY HAVE FALLEN

The comments in the media at the end of this exciting and fascinating World Formula 1 Championship could more or less have been inspired by the film *La Caduta degli Dei (The Damned/Die Götterdämmerung)* by Luchino Visconti. Oh, how the mighty, that is the god Schumacher and the god Ferrari, have fallen! After what seemed like an eternity of total domination and supremacy, the likes of which will probably never be seen again in Formula 1, the invincible Italo-German armada was finally ousted from the throne.

It was a year of suffering for the Prancing Horse team, which only had one win to celebrate, at Indianapolis after the disaster that befell tyre manufacturer Michelin.

There are probably three reasons for this dramatic U-turn in fortune:

The improvement made by Ferrari's rivals, Renault and McLaren; the change in the points system; the compulsory use of one set of tyres throughout the weekend and as a result, the abolition of pit-stops.

While the improvement of Ferrari's rivals was the direct result of the competitiveness of today's Formula 1, it is worth pointing out that since 2003 Ferrari has been the driving-force behind the evolution in the FIA technical and sporting regulations aimed at counter-balancing their own supremacy.

From a sporting point of view, in 2003 a gap of just two points between Schumacher and Raikkonen (93 to 91) in the final standings was not reflected in the actual win difference between the two drivers: the German scoring six to the Finn's one. This goes to prove that the when the rules are made, they should be made for no one in particular……

This year the big difference basically regards the performance of Ferrari, the only top team to use non-Michelin rubber.

Chief rivals Fernando Alonso and Kimi Raikkonen, together with their respective Renault and McLaren teams, finally had an opportunity to fight for the title because they were faced with a suddenly uncompetitive Ferrari.

This was the big surprise of the season and it basically stemmed from the fact that the new regulations imposed the use of one set of tyres for the entire race weekend. In the past Bridgestone's contribution to the success of Ferrari had been fundamental. In 2005 however these new regulations totally modified Ferrari's performance and the blame for this lies with the Japanese tyre manufacturer.

A critical analysis however cannot ignore a more complex appraisal of the technical design of the car to see whether or not something had changed in Ferrari's working method to lead to this drop in performance. There were some defections from the aerodynamics sector as well as some internal changes within Ferrari, but this does not explain the Prancing Horse's fall from grace.

Ferrari's hard-core engineering staff remained exactly the same (Ross Brawn, Rory Byrne and Paolo Martinelli) and Aldo Costa was given more responsibility in view of the eventual departure of Rory Byrne.

When a team is in the middle of a crisis, thoughts turn to all sorts of reasons for the poor performance: potential errors in the car design, excessive stiffness in the rear suspension, not enough downforce, the need for a more powerful engine, and so on.

If the problems are identified, it is unreasonable to think that the Maranello staff are not capable of reacting to resolve those problems. After the first few races, when it was clear that Ferrari were in difficulty, Ross Brawn admitted that Ferrari had to begin to modify the 'concept' of the car and the tyre as it had been viewed until now to respond to the requirements brought about by a one-race tyre.

To say that the reason for Ferrari's poor performance this year was the tyre and that its performance over a race weekend was inferior to its Michelin rival, is true but just to a certain point.

It is true that Bridgestone were unable to produce a tyre for the car that was efficient and performed well enough in any track conditions; throughout the year in fact the Japanese struggled to gain that fine balance between tread wear and outright performance. Whenever one diminished so did the other and in the end they were unable to fathom out the reason why.

Ferrari were also not in a position to help their partner find a solution to the problems. Just like the problems that Michelin encountered when they first returned to Formula 1, the number of rival teams supplied with tyres proved to be so much of an advantage that Dupasquier and company found it easier to design a one-race tyre due to the sheer quantity of statistical and technical information available.

In the 2005 season mention must also be made of the safety aspect associated with the one-race tyre. Virtually every driver had to face a critical situation throughout the year but things dramatically came to a head with the withdrawal of the Michelin teams from the Indianapolis race.

If we ignore this tremendous blow to Formula 1's image in general, it is clear that the regulation is far too restrictive to be applied in the long term because of the sheer risk involved. A case in point is the suspension failure on Raikkonen's McLaren at the Nurburgring, which came about because the rules do not allow a tyre change during the race.

It must also be mentioned that pit stops just for refuelling purposes proved to be rather unspectacular.

Finally a word about the splendid season for Renault and its driver Fernando Alonso. It is a young and victorious partnership, one that will surely be a shining-star in Formula 1 for a long time. Just three years after their full-time return to Formula 1, Renault have achieved success with the conquest of the Drivers' and Constructors' titles, the result of the extraordinary work carried out by Patrick Faure and Flavio Briatore, both champions in their own special way!

Giorgio Stirano

CALENDAR
Formula 1 - 2005

A desert backdrop for the official launch of the new Williams F1 car in its 2005 livery, highlighting a new major sponsor – the Royal Bank of Scotland. Present at the launch were the team's new signing Mark Webber, together with Antonio Pizzonia, a possible candidate for the number 2 drive, even though it looks as if Nick Heidfeld will probably get the drive.

January 6
Bahrain

November 15 - 2004

Jaguar, which forms part of the Ford Group, finally bids farewell to the F1 circus after five years and a series of disappointing results. Its place on the grid is taken by Red Bull, the multinational energy drink company belonging to Austrian Dietrich Mateschitz. The sale is reported to have gone ahead for the symbolic price of 1 dollar but with a precise commitment by Red Bull to take over the squad and the machinery and to guarantee the full activity of the former Jaguar team for at least three years.

January 14 - Valencia

The new Sauber C24 was due to have been launched in Kuala Lumpur, home of Malaysian sponsor Petronas, celebrating ten years of Formula 1 collaboration, but the tsunami tragedy forced the team to present the car at the Valencia circuit.

January 16
Barcelona

The BAR Honda 007, presented by new team manager Nick Fry together with top Honda management, took to the track. From 2005 Honda have a major presence in the team as 45% shareholder and probably intend to take over the majority at the end of the year.

January 20

Sid Watkins, the FIA's Chief Medical Officer for 26 years and one of Formula 1's legendary figures, leaves the sport for good. His position aboard the Mercedes FIA Medical Car, which is present at every GP, goes to his assistant, Gary Hartstein. Sid Watkins, a world-famous neurosurgeon, was born in England in 1928 and graduated from Oxford University.

68

January 24

Eddie Jordan sold off the team bearing his name to the Midland Group, belonging to Russian millionaire Alex Shnaider. Shnaider has for some time now been considering entering F1 and had actually started on the construction of a brand-new car with the collaboration of Dallara.

January - Jerez

David Coulthard, 34 years old and 175 GPs to his name, takes over behind the wheel of the new Cosworth-powered Red Bull RB1 at the Jerez circuit in Spain. The ex-Stewart and ex-Jaguar car is an evolution version of the 2004 Jaguar. The new team had far too little time to make any substantial modifications, but the new sponsor's livery is splendid.

February 25 - Maranello

In line with years of tradition, the new F2005 is presented to international media at Ferrari headquarters in Maranello. The launch is a particularly exciting one for Aldo Costa, the engineer who designed the car and the first Italian to do so since the legendary Mauro Forghieri. After 6 Constructors' titles and 5 successive Drivers' titles, Costa has a tough act to follow.

February 25
Moscow

While the world's media are watching Schumacher & Co. unveil the new F2005 at Maranello, a freezing cold Red Square in Moscow was the scene for the launch of the new Jordan, which now belongs to the Russian tycoon Alex Shnaider. Eddie Jordan, taking probably the final curtain in his long F1 career, was present together with two of the sport's biggest names, Bernie Ecclestone and Flavio Briatore.

April 17
Rome

Despite a sudden downpour that flooded the track set up around the spectacular Circus Maximus in Rome, 25,000 fans were able to cheer on local hero, Giancarlo Fisichella, in his Renault F1 car.

April 21 - Imola

Shell and Ferrari announced a renewal of their collaboration agreement until 2010. Shell has been partner to the Maranello cars as sponsor and fuel supplier since 1996, but the prestigious 'shell' logo also emblazoned the Prancing Horse cars and the first team trucks back in the 1950s.

April 21
Imola

After the massive McLaren motorhome which was inaugurated in 2003, once again the Imola circuit was the scene for the presentation of the extraordinary Red Bull structure. More than ten trucks are required to transport the team's motorhome.

April 24
Mugello

The first V8 engine, which will become obligatory in 2006, made a rather low-profile track debut at Mugello. Anthony Davidson did the driving duties with an old BAR chassis fitted with a Honda V8.

April 22
Imola

Once again the CEA fire-fighters were present at the Imola circuit for the 25th San Marino Formula 1 Grand Prix. The Bologna firm, one of the world leaders in fire-fighting, provided 200 specialised staff and 31 fully-equipped rapid-intervention vehicles for the GP, including a Ferrari 348, 5 Alfa Romeos and 3 Land Rovers. These cars were backed up by two multi-function vehicles fitted with equipment for extracting a driver from a damaged cockpit.

May 5
Paris

For the first time in the history of Formula 1 a team was disqualified for three races following an FIA Appeals Court ruling. It happened to BAR, who were found guilty of fuel irregularities (basically a hidden extra fuel tank containing 9 kilograms of fuel). At scrutineering the car weighed more than the 600 kg limit stipulated by the regulations but it is clear that the 9 kg of extra fuel allowed the British cars both to complete more laps than their rivals and to have a lower weight for much of the race.

June 5

Balbiz Singh, Michael Schumacher's physiotherapist, dietician, friend and guru for the last ten years, decides to return back home to India at the end of the season to spend more time with his family.

June 22

Munich

Burkhard Göschel and Mario Theissen of BMW announced they had reached an agreement with the Sauber shareholders (Peter Sauber and Credit Suisse) for the takeover of the Swiss F1 team. From January 1, 2006 BMW will enter a team under its own name in the championship and no longer as engine supplier to Williams. The future of BMW's rapport with Williams, which began back in 2000, is still to be defined.

July 10

David Coulthard renews his contract with Red Bull, which will have Ferrari engines and Bridgestone tyres, for 2006.

July 19

Minardi announce that Dutchman Robert Doornbos will take over from Patrick Friesacher from the German GP onwards.

July 31
Budapest

Toyota also confirmed the supply of engines to Jordan for 2006. The agreement will in all likelihood come to an conclusion at the end of the season because for 2007 the Japanese V8 engine will probably be fitted to the Williams.

August 2
Maranello

Ferrari and Barrichello announce their divorce, after six seasons spent together which produced 9 wins, 61 podiums and 13 pole positions. At the end of the season Rubens will become a BAR driver while another Brazilian, 24-year-old Felipe Massa, 34 GPs to his name, is to join Ferrari as their second driver in 2006.

August 28 - Oschersleben

Incredible but true … as Alex Zanardi won a race again! In the seventh round of the World Touring Car Championship at Oschersleben, not far away from the Lausitzring circuit where four years ago he had his dramatic crash, Alex dominated race 2 to step onto the top of the podium. The last few laps were full of emotion as the crowd cheered him on while he held off Andy Priaulx for the win.

September 20

Nick Heidfeld will become a BMW-Sauber driver in 2006 after Williams decided not to take up their option on the German.

September 10

Red Bull announced that it had bought up the Minardi Team owned by Paul Stoddart.

minardi F1 team

September 25
Brazil

Schumacher and Barrichello celebrated 100 GPs together at Interlagos. The previous record belonged to the legendary McLaren pairing of Hakkinen and Coulthard, who raced together for 98 GPs.

September 26
Brazil

Fernando Alonso became the youngest-ever world champion in the history of Formula 1 at the age of 24 years and 58 days. The previous record belonged to Emerson Fittipaldi. It was also the first-ever world title for Renault as a team.

October 16
Shanghai

The last race of the year was also the time for several farewells. The 10 cylinder engines were taken away to the museums, to be replaced by new V8 power-units. Peter Sauber, the Swiss gentleman of Formula 1, stepped down as the head of the team he founded, which has now been bought up by BMW. Paul Stoddart, the curious European-Australian owner of Minardi, said goodbye to Formula 1 after he sold the former Italian outfit to Red Bull, which will run it as its second F1 team. It was all change over at BAR as well, as the Japanese Honda giant officially moved into Formula 1 after taking over full ownership of the team.

Tiago Monteiro
Jordan's Portuguese driver started racing quite late, at the age of 20, in the Porsche Carrera series in France. After four years of French F3 he moved up to F3000 with the Supernova team and then went to the USA for the Champ Car series before arriving in F1.

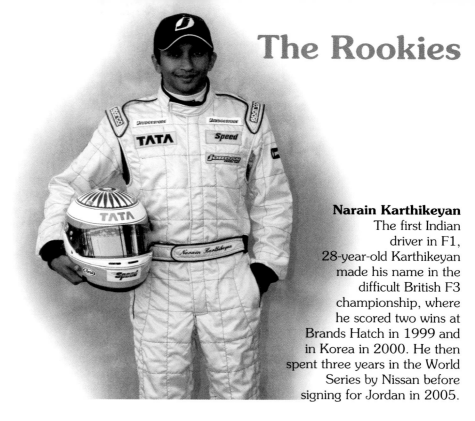

Narain Karthikeyan
The first Indian driver in F1, 28-year-old Karthikeyan made his name in the difficult British F3 championship, where he scored two wins at Brands Hatch in 1999 and in Korea in 2000. He then spent three years in the World Series by Nissan before signing for Jordan in 2005.

Patrick Friesacher
Thanks to financial backing from Red Bull, Friesacher has succeeded in moving from the Formula Campus championship in France to F3 and then into F3000, winning the Hungaroring race at the end of 2004. Speaks four languages perfectly.

Vitantonio Liuzzi
His contract with Sauber is 'part-time' but at least he will have the opportunity to make his name known to the world of F1. Liuzzi won the world karting championship in 2001 and raced in Formula Renault and in F3000 in 2003 with the Coloni team, winning the championship the following year with Arden.

Robert Doornbos
The 24-year-old Dutchman began his racing career in 1999 with an Opel Lotus in the British Winter Series. He was snapped up by Jordan as test-driver at the end of the 2004 season.

Christijan Albers
The best Dutch driver since the retirement of Jos Verstappen, Albers began his career in karting before moving into Formula Ford, F3, F3000 and then onto the DTM, the German Touring Car Championship, with Mercedes. He has already tested a Minardi in 2001 and 2002.

Fernando Alonso

Date of birth: 29 July 1981
Oviedo (Spain)
F1 debut: Australian GP 2001

Year	Team	GP	Points	Pole	Victories
1991					
1992					
1993					
1994					
1995					
1996					
1997					
1998					
1999					
2000					
2001	Minardi	-	-	-	-
2002					
2003	Renault	16	55	2	1
2004	Renault	18	59	1	-

Giancarlo Fisichella

Date of birth: 14 January 1973
Roma (Italy)
F1 debut: Australian GP 1996

Year	Team	GP	Points	Pole	Victories
1991					
1992					
1993					
1994					
1995					
1996	Minardi-Ford	8	-	-	-
1997	Jordan-Peugeot	17	20	-	-
1998	Benetton-Playlife	16	16	1	-
1999	Benetton-Playlife	16	13	-	-
2000	Benetton-Playlife	17	18	-	-
2001	Benetton-Renault	17	8	-	-
2002	Jordan	16	7	-	-
2003	Sauber-Petronas	16	12	-	1
2004	Sauber-Petronas	18	22	-	-

Kimi Raikkonen

Date of birth: 17 October 1979
Espoo (Finland)
F1 debut: Australian GP 2001

Year	Team	GP	Points	Pole	Victories
1991					
1992					
1993					
1994					
1995					
1996					
1997					
1998					
1999					
2000					
2001	Sauber-Petronas	16	9	-	-
2002	McLaren-Mercedes	17	24	-	-
2003	McLaren-Mercedes	16	91	2	1
2004	McLaren-Mercedes	18	45	1	1

Juan Pablo Montoya

Date of birth: 20 September 1975
Bogotà (Colombia)
F1 debut: Australian GP 2001

Year	Team	GP	Points	Pole	Victories
1991					
1992					
1993					
1994					
1995					
1996					
1997					
1998					
1999					
2000					
2001	Williams-BMW	17	31	1	1
2002	Williams-BMW	17	50	7	-
2003	Williams-BMW	16	82	1	2
2004	Williams-BMW	18	58	-	1

Michael Schumacher

Date of birth: 3 January 1969
Hurt-Hermulheim (Germany)
F1 debut: Belgian GP 1991

Year	Team	GP	Points	Pole	Victories
1991	Jordan/Benetton-Ford	6	4	-	-
1992	Benetton-Ford	16	53	-	1
1993	Benetton-Ford	16	52	-	1
1994	Benetton-Ford	14	92	6	8
1995	Benetton-Renault	17	102	4	9
1996	Ferrari	15	59	4	3
1997	Ferrari	17	78	3	5
1998	Ferrari	16	86	3	6
1999	Ferrari	9	44	3	2
2000	Ferrari	17	108	9	9
2001	Ferrari	17	123	11	9
2002	Ferrari	17	144	7	11
2003	Ferrari	16	93	5	6
2004	Ferrari	18	148	8	13

Rubens Barrichello

Date of birth: 23 May 1972
Sao Paolo (Brazil)
F1 debut: Brazilian GP 1993

Year	Team	GP	Points	Pole	Victories
1991					
1992					
1993	Jordan-Hart	16	2	-	-
1994	Jordan-Hart	15	19	1	-
1995	Jordan-Peugeot	17	11	-	-
1996	Jordan-Peugeot	16	14	-	-
1997	Stewart-Ford	17	6	-	-
1998	Stewart-Ford	15	4	-	-
1999	Stewart-Ford	16	21	1	-
2000	Ferrari	17	62	1	1
2001	Ferrari	17	56	-	-
2002	Ferrari	17	77	3	4
2003	Ferrari	16	65	3	2
2004	Ferrari	18	114	4	2

Jarno Trulli

Date of birth: 13 July 1974
Pescara (Italy)
F1 debut: Australian GP 1997

Year	Team	GP	Points	Pole	Victories
1991					
1992					
1993					
1994					
1995					
1996					
1997	Minardi-Prost	14	3	-	-
1998	Prost-Peugeot	16	1	-	-
1999	Prost-Peugeot	15	7	-	-
2000	Jordan-Mugen	17	6	-	-
2001	Jordan-Honda	17	12	-	-
2002	Renault	17	9	-	-
2003	Renault	16	33	-	-
2004	Toyota	17	46	2	1

Ralf Schumacher

Date of birth: 30 June 1975
Hurt-Hermulheim (Germany)
F1 debut: Australian GP 1997

Year	Team	GP	Points	Pole	Victories
1991					
1992					
1993					
1994					
1995					
1996					
1997	Jordan-Peugeot	17	13	-	-
1998	Jordan-Mugen	16	14	-	-
1999	Williams-Supertec	16	35	-	-
2000	Williams-BMW	17	24	-	-
2001	Williams-BMW	17	49	1	3
2002	Williams-BMW	17	42	-	1
2003	Williams-BMW	15	58	3	2
2004	Williams-BMW	12	24	1	-

Jenson Button

Date of birth: 19 January 1980
Frome, Somerset (England)
F1 debut: Australian GP 2000

Year	Team	GP	Points	Pole	Victories
1991					
1992					
1993					
1994					
1995					
1996					
1997					
1998					
1999					
2000	Williams-BMW	17	12	-	-
2001	Benetton-Renault	17	2	-	-
2002	Renault	17	14	-	-
2003	BAR-Honda	15	17	-	-
2004	BAR-Honda	18	85	1	-

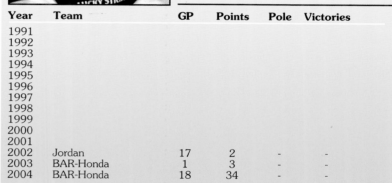

Takuma Sato

Date of birth: 28 January 1977
Tokyo (Japan)
F1 debut: Australian GP 2002

Year	Team	GP	Points	Pole	Victories
1991					
1992					
1993					
1994					
1995					
1996					
1997					
1998					
1999					
2000					
2001					
2002	Jordan	17	2	-	-
2003	BAR-Honda	1	3	-	-
2004	BAR-Honda	18	34	-	-

Mark Webber

Date of birth: 27 August 1976
Queanbeyan (Australia)
F1 debut: Australian GP 2002

Year	Team	GP	Points	Pole	Victories
1991					
1992					
1993					
1994					
1995					
1996					
1997					
1998					
1999					
2000					
2001					
2002	Minardi	16	2	-	-
2003	Jaguar	16	17	-	-
2004	Jaguar	18	7	-	-

Nick Heidfeld

Date of birth: 10 May 1977
Monchengladbach (Germany)
F1 debut: Australian GP 2000

Year	Team	GP	Points	Pole	Victories
1991					
1992					
1993					
1994					
1995					
1996					
1997					
1998					
1999					
2000	Prost-Peugeot	16	-	-	-
2001	Sauber-Petronas	17	12	-	-
2002	Sauber-Petronas	17	7	-	-
2003	Sauber-Petronas	16	6	-	-
2004	Jordan	18	3	-	-

David Coulthard

Date of birth: 27 March 1971
Twynholm (Scotland)
F1 debut: Spanish GP 1994

Year	Team	GP	Points	Pole	Victories
1991					
1992					
1993					
1994	Williams-Renault	8	14	-	-
1995	Williams-Renault	17	49	5	1
1996	McLaren-Mercedes	16	18	-	-
1997	McLaren-Mercedes	17	36		2
1998	McLaren-Mercedes	16	56	3	1
1999	McLaren-Mercedes	16	48	-	2
2000	McLaren-Mercedes	17	73	2	3
2001	McLaren-Mercedes	17	65	2	2
2002	McLaren-Mercedes	17	41	-	1
2003	McLaren-Mercedes	16	51	-	1
2004	McLaren-Mercedes	18	24	-	-

Christian Klien

Date of birth: 7 February 1983
Hohenems (Austria)
F1 debut: Australian GP 2004

Year	Team	GP	Points	Pole	Victories
2004	Jaguar	18	3	-	-

Jacques Villeneuve

Date of birth: 9 April 1971
St. Jean-sur-Richelieu (Canada)
F1 debut: Australian GP 1996

Year	Team	GP	Points	Pole	Victories
1991					
1992					
1993					
1994					
1995					
1996	Williams-Renault	16	78	3	4
1997	Williams-Renault	17	81	10	7
1998	Williams-Mecachrome	16	21	-	-
1999	BAR-Supertec	16	-	-	-
2000	BAR-Honda	17	17	-	-
2001	BAR-Honda	17	12	-	-
2002	BAR-Honda	17	4	-	-
2003	BAR-Honda	15	6	-	-
2004	Renault	3	-	-	-

Felipe Massa

Date of birth: 25 April 1981
Sao Paolo (Brazil)
F1 debut: Australian GP 2002

Year	Team	GP	Points	Pole	Victories
1991					
1992					
1993					
1994					
1995					
1996					
1997					
1998					
1999					
2000					
2001					
2002	Sauber-Petronas	16	4	-	-
2003					
2004	Sauber-Petronas	18	12	-	-

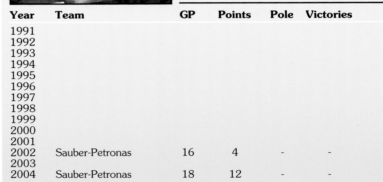

Narain Karthikeyan

Date of birth: 14 January 1977
Madras (India)
F1 debut: Australian GP 2005

Tiago Monteiro

Date of birth: 24 July 1976
Oporto (Portugal)
F1 debut: Australian GP 2005

Christijan Albers

Date of birth: 16 April 1979
Eindhoven (Netherland)
F1 debut: Australian GP 2005

Robert Doornbos

Date of birth: 23 September 1981
Rotterdam (Netherland)
F1 debut: German GP 2005

Patrick Friesacher

Date of birth: 26 September 1980
Wolsberg (Austria)
F1 debut: Australian GP 2005

Anthony Davidson

Date of birth: 18 April 1979
Hemel Hempstead (England)
F1 debut: Hungarian GP 2002

Pedro De La Rosa

Date of birth: 24 February 1971
Barcelona (Spain)
F1 debut: Australian GP 1999

Alexander Wurz

Date of birth: 15 February 1974
Waidhofen (Austria)
F1 debut: Canadian GP 1997

Vitantonio Liuzzi

Date of birth: 6 August 1981
Locorotondo (Bari-Italy)
F1 debut: San Marino GP 2005

Antonio Pizzonia

Date of birth:11 September 1980
Manaus (Brazil)
F1 debut: Australian GP 2003

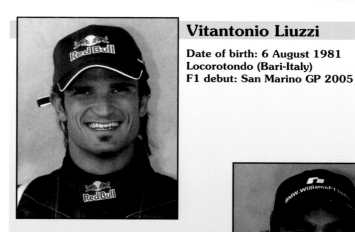

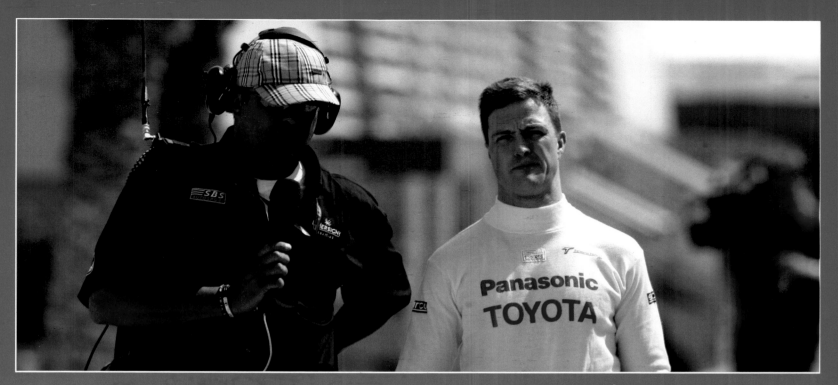

83

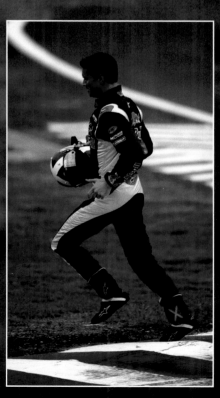

2005 FORMULA 1:
A CHANGE IN THE BALANCE

by Paolo D'ALESSIO

Sooner or later Ferrari's domination of Formula 1 had to come to an end, but not even their worst enemies could have envisaged such a difficult season for the Prancing Horse team. In the space of just a few months the Italian cars went from almost total domination to almost total embarrassment, from being the sport's top team to just making up the numbers. It was an unmitigated disaster that disappointed millions of fans throughout the world, and those very same fans continue to wonder how it was possible for Ferrari to go from the fifteen wins of the past season to the embarrassment of the 2005 world championship.

The obvious tendency is to lay the blame at the foot of Japanese tyre supplier Bridgestone, but this would neither be true nor entirely accurate. The reasons for Ferrari's crisis are actually more complex and complicated; they range from the team's 'isolation' at the very moment in which it became Bridgestone's only real point of reference, to the continuous changes in the regulations, which did it no favours, the down-sizing of the racing department (from 820 employees in 2004 to 750 in 2005) and the departure of key engineers from the aerodynamics (Tombazis) and electronics (Stipinovich) sectors.

If all these elements are combined, it becomes easy to see how the invincible Ferrari armada of the previous seasons, can rapidly sink to the bottom of the F1 ocean. Luckily for Maranello, in 2006 the regulations will change once again (the current three litre V10s will become 2.4 litre eight cylinder engines) and the Italian team will again be able to count on a highly-motivated Michael Schumacher, who anxious to make amends for his terrible year.

While Ferrari was on the way down, Renault and McLaren were rapidly moving in the opposite direction, irrespective of their actual results. Right from the start of the 2004 season it was clear that the performances of both Renault and McLaren were improving. The Flavio Briatore-led team, which won at Monte Carlo last year with Trulli, finally managed to emerge from the technical status quo represented by its 111° V10 engine. The 72° V10 unit that made its debut in the R24 might not have been as powerful as the Ferrari, but it certainly made up for that by being reliable. McLaren, which had shaken off the disappointment of the MP4/18 and the first version of the MP4/19, was returning to competitive form once again after sacrificing outright performance and sheer geniality. Take two potentially victorious cars, develop them six months ahead of the competition (i.e. Ferrari) in view of the new regulations, fit them with unbeatable Michelin tyres, and there you have it.

This was basically the secret that helped Renault and McLaren fight for the world title during the year and allowed them to oust Ferrari from its throne. Obviously each of these two teams had its own particular way of reaching the top. The Alonso-Renault pairing took the conservative route by preferring to administrate the considerable advantage it had accumulated in the first few GPs of the year, when its rivals were struggling with new car set-up and getting to grips with still rather vague regulations. The McLaren phenomenon burst into life in the second part of the season, when after reaching an acceptable (but not perfect) level of reliability, the Adrian Newey designed car demonstrated on the track the potential that had remained unfulfilled for the past couple of seasons. That was the start of a run of victories and a sequence of incredible performances by the McLaren-Mercedes pairing, culminating in the top speed of 371 km/h reached by Montoya at Monza.

Unlike the past season, when the gap between Ferrari and the rest had been embarrassing, the 2005 championship was much more even and threw up a series of new names to watch for the future, in particular the two Japanese teams, BAR and Toyota.

After shrugging off a disqualification for the use of an illegal fuel tank, Jenson Button started to appear regularly in the top positions, and even though his BAR was not as competitive as the previous season, it will surely become so in 2006 when the new V8, the arrival of Barrichello and the full takeover of the team by Honda mean that its chances of success will improve considerably. The same can be said for Toyota, which began the season with the disastrous TF105 but thanks to Jarno Trulli (quick in qualifying and an excellent test-driver) and a constant updating of the car, they ended the season on a high note.

Two more names to watch out for in 2006 are Sauber and Red Bull. Twelve years after entering Formula 1 with Mercedes, the Swiss constructor capitulated to an offer made by BMW. The German manufacturer dropped the increasingly uncompetitive Williams team, bought up the Hinvil-based squad and will now build everything in-house, from chassis to engine.

Renault's lengthy learning curve should be a warning, but BMW are certainly not lacking in resources. Neither are they short of funds over at Red Bull (ex-Jaguar), which to be honest were the real surprise of 2005. Many people thought that the acquisition of Ford's former racing department by the energy drink producer was just a publicity stunt. Yet, with a relatively simple but reliable car and an expert driver of the calibre of David Coulthard, Red Bull scored more points in one year that Jaguar had done in the previous seasons. And just to put the icing on the cake, the Red Bull owner also managed to negotiate a supply of new Ferrari 2.4 litre V8 engines and the purchase of Minardi, which from 2006 onwards will become a sort of Red Bull junior team, aimed at launching new talent in GP racing.

Not bad going in a period of worldwide economic crisis...

RENAULT R25

That the Renault R25 was destined for success, could be seen right from the first day the 2005 car took to the track, when Fernando Alonso and Giancarlo Fisichella required just a few laps to declare that it had excellent potential. Few observers however were prepared to give much credit to Flavio Briatore's team, which had smashed all records during winter testing, but when the R25 monopolized the front row of the grid and the highest podium position at the opening round of the season in Melbourne, Australia, no lingering doubts remained. The Renault was the revelation of 2005 and it would continue that way for the first four rounds on the calendar, which concluded with four wins for the Anglo-French car. People were beginning to wonder what was so innovative and revolutionary in a car that last year had alternated between good results and poor races; or, if you prefer, in a car that finished the 2004 constructors' championship in third place, but 157 points behind the dominating Ferrari. Yet part of the R25's success depended on Ferrari. After they had realised that it was impossible to beat the F2004, engineers at Enstone halted all development of the R24 from the summer of 2004, and concentrated exclusively on the car destined for the 2005 season, when new FIA rules would be introduced.

The result was a car that has clear links with the previous model, but also a series of innovations, developed by the Enstone team. The real strong point of the R25 was its aerodynamics package. In 2005 Renault engineers were not inspired either by the Ferrari's spoon-shaped nose or the Sauber's and McLaren's twin keel, instead they opted for an extreme tapered front and for a brand-new lower wishbone suspension mounting system (a V profile in carbon, anchored under the frame), which allowed a greater quantity of air to be channelled under the body and thus regain some of the downforce that had been lost with the entry into force of the new regulations. Inspired by the Ferrari F2003 GA's sides, which were tapered and hollowed out to the rear, Enstone engineers further exasperated this concept by creating smaller and much more rounded sidepods. On top of these, the traditional vents for the hot air were replaced by a series of slits or 'gills' which had a dual function: to lower the temperature inside the sidepods and speed up the flow of air to the rear wing. This was an idea that came from the Ferrari F2003 GA, but it was developed by Briatore's team and exasperated in view of the new regulations. However good the aerodynamics might be on a Formula 1 car, they are not enough to guarantee success on the track. On the R25, like most of today's top Formula 1 cars, success also comes from the ability to integrate the various elements and make them interact with each other. In the case of Alonso's and Fisichella's cars the domination of the first part of the championship was also determined by a perfect integration of the latest Michelin tyres with the R25's suspension and by a different weight distribution to last year's car, with a division that now had slightly more balance over the front axle. Alonso and Fisichella also benefited from the best traction control system on the grid, which throughout the season allowed them to preserve their Michelin radials and conclude the races with tyres that were still in good shape. Another winning secret of the R25 was its Renault engine. The latest version of the French power-unit amazed everyone with its performance and reliability, especially considering the fact that twelve months ago it was indicated as one of the weak points of the team. Also in this case Renault went its own way, developing a ten cylinder unit that bucked the trend, with a narrow Vee angle of just 72°. Its power output was inferior to that of the Mercedes V10, but in return it proved to be indestructible. It is a well-known fact that to have a chance of aiming for the title, reliability is one of the most important factors.

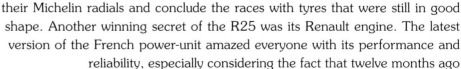

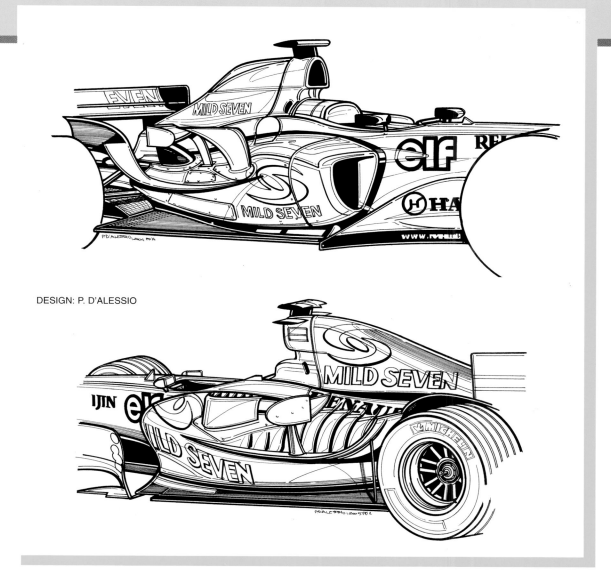

DESIGN: P. D'ALESSIO

The sides of the Renault R25 are characterized by marked rear tapering, as well as a pronounced opening in the lower part of the sidepods, inherited from the Ferrari F2003 GA. The 2005 Renault differed from last year's car (see above alongside) in the layered pattern of the bodywork. The expulsion of the heat from inside the sidepods (hot air from the engine and the radiators) came through the 'shark's gills', a series of deep transversal slits across the upper part of the bodywork, and they also helped to speed up the flow of air to the rear wing, which regulations allowed to be located further forward.

The exasperated 'spoon-shaped' front wing (see below) and a narrower nose compensated for the loss of front-end downforce. With the nose removed, the R25 revealed its innovative front end (see below right). In order to channel a greater quantity of air under the car and increase downforce over the front axle, Renault engineers anchored the lower wishbone mounting of the front suspension to a Vee-shaped carbon structure, which also acted as a flow guide for the air that found its way into the underbody.

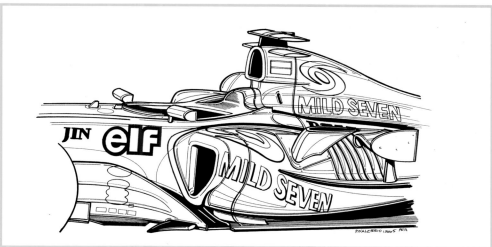

RENAULT R25

Comparison between the 2004 Renault (see above) and the 2005 car (see alongside). The exasperated spoon-shaped front wing, together with a brand-new front suspension mounting, reduced the loss of downforce on the front axle, while the narrower nose helped to channel a greater quantity of air under the car, increasing ground effect. With a car that was now generating more downforce, Renault also succeeded in minimizing the loss by locating the rear wing further forward and by resizing the rear diffuser. The sides were also resized and those on the R25 had a strong downward tapering. Inside (as can be noticed in the cross-section), they housed high-performance radiant masses that were even smaller than those on the R24, which considerably improved the car's fluid dynamics.

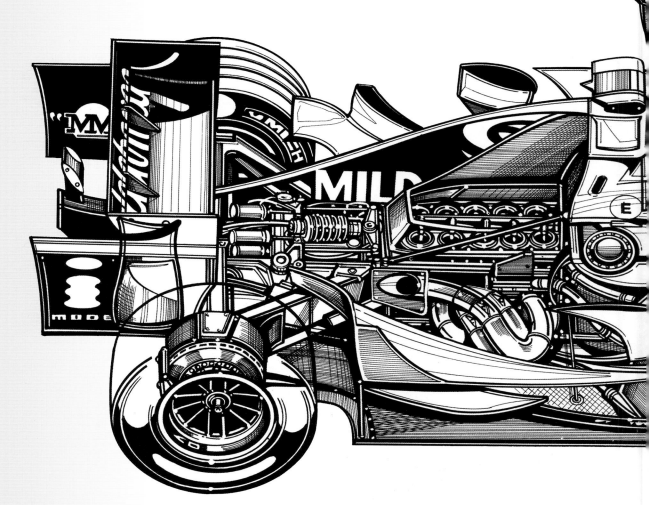

Anyone who thought that the weak link in
the Renault R25 package was the engine had
to think again: in 2005 Renault closed the gap
to its rivals both in performance and in reliability.
The key difference was in the French engine's
architecture, which was the only ten-cylinder unit
on the grid to have a 72° Vee angle. This particular
architecture had been in fashion during the turbo era,
but it was abandoned because it was not suitable for
a lower centre of gravity, which was absolutely vital
for the set-up of modern Formula 1 cars with
their narrow track and grooved tyres.

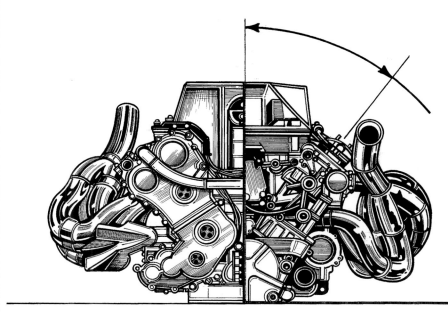

Renault were able to win, even though
according to Flavio Briatore "the R25's
ten-cylinder engine (see design above)
should weigh about 15 kilos more
with respect to the best engine around
(the Mercedes V10) and above
all have about 40 HP less
than the German unit".

DESIGN: P. D'ALESSIO

117

McLAREN MERCEDES MP4/20

The McLaren-Mercedes MP4/20 was undoubtedly the best car of 2005. All credit for this must go to Adrian Newey, Formula 1's unrestrained genius and to Nick Tombazis, who for the past few years has been Ferrari's aerodynamics expert. They created an extreme package, a car that was drop-dead gorgeous and extraordinarily efficient at the same time. Once teething problems had been sorted out, the MP4/20 was unbeatable both on medium-slow tracks like the Hungaroring and on fast ones like Silverstone. It was a shame that the silver cars only returned to form from the Spanish GP onwards, when Alonso and Renault had already piled up a sizeable points lead. Until then the Ron Dennis-run team had been paying for the errors of previous seasons. The errors began in 2003, when McLaren introduced the MP4/18 in the midst of the championship battle with Ferrari after starting the season with the MP4/17D. The new car, as extreme as all of the Newey-designed cars were, was a total failure. Around 50 million Euro were wasted in trying to make the car competitive, but Newey didn't give in and in 2004 he dusted down the same concepts for the MP4/19. This was also a complete failure, at least until the 2004 French GP, when the B version was introduced and it went on to win the Belgian GP with Raikkonen. 2005's MP4/20 derived from that model and it became unbeatable from the San Marino GP, when a new aerodynamics package and new front suspension were introduced.

To get back to the top, Adrian Newey had to abandon several key features of the 2003/4 McLaren cars, features in which he blindly believed, such as the twin-keel, where the front suspension was anchored, or the narrow nose, which had proved effective in the wind-tunnel but not so good on the track. The 2005 McLaren sported the same wide 'ant-eater' nose that made its debut on the MP4/19 last year at Monza, and a hybrid suspension mount. The MP4/20 abandoned the twin-keel, but used lateral barge-boards that were fitted directly to the sides of the car body to channel a greater amount of air into the car and increase downforce. Another winning feature of the 2005 McLaren was the neat design of the sides, clearly inspired by Ferrari. On the MP4/20 Newey and Tombazis exasperated the F2003 GA's low 'waistline' in view of the new rules. In addition, the McLaren designers modified the shape and size of the barge-boards to wipe out the aerodynamic block that had been a feature of the previous McLarens. The result was that the MP4/20 went like a rocket in the fast curves and on the straights Raikkonen and Montoya were simply the quickest drivers in the field.

The MP4/20's neat aerodynamics, combined with a modified cooling system (high-efficiency radiators, inclined inside the sidepods) helped to make the McLarens the quickest cars around. But the resurrection of the Silver Arrows would not have been possible without a competitive power-unit and this was the FO110R, the revised Mercedes engine for 2005. The German power-unit now had a superb horsepower range, like it had had in previous years, and easily made amends for its poor 2004 performance. It was only a partial success however because although the Mercedes 10 cylinder engine became the most powerful on the grid from the British GP onwards (the first fast circuit of the year), reliability was still McLaren's Achilles Heel. Far too often they were forced to retire from the race or were relegated ten places down on the starting-grid due to mechanical problems. Another winning feature of the McLaren MP4/20 was its perfect marriage with the Michelin tyres. From the Spanish GP, with the introduction of the latest modifications to the innovative front suspension, Raikkonen and Montoya's cars became Michelin's key reference point and the ones that used the French radial tyres in the best way. More well-balanced than the Renault, the MP4/20 did not slide around in the corners and consumed the tyres in a more gradual and constant way. This was an important detail in a world championship dominated by tyres.

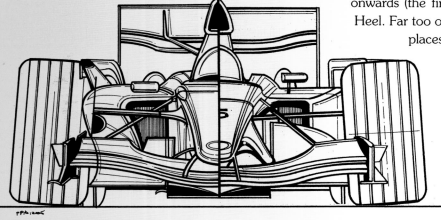

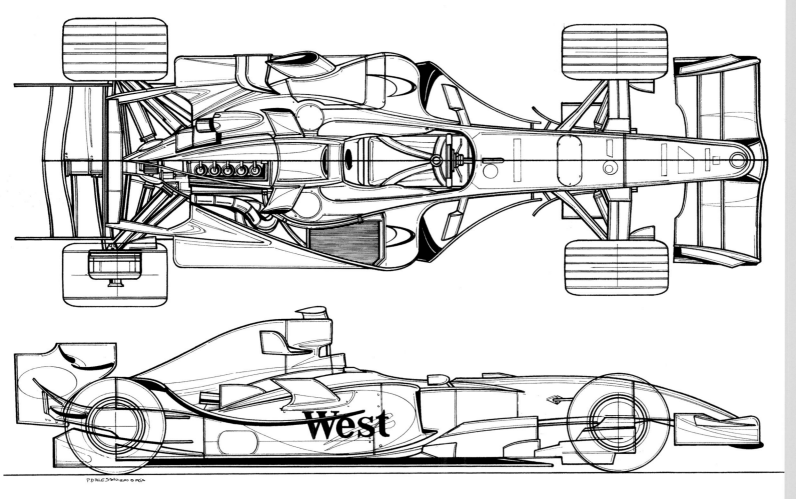

DESIGN: P. D'ALESSIO

The McLaren MP4/20 had extremely small sides. To improve air flow on the outside of the sidepods and increase downforce, Adrian Newey and Nick Tombazis redesigned the sides of the MP4/20 (see below, the comparison with the MP4/19). The sidepods on the 2005 McLaren are even shorter and more rounded than the previous versions and had a triangular shape, with a tightening of the 'waistline' in the lower part. The sides of the MP4/20 are also characterized by having a sharp drop towards the rear. The smaller size of the sides at the rear was emphasized by a higher and steeper engine air intake, and by an unprecedented rear tapering. As can be seen in the side view and the plan, there are several original solutions such as the low, flat 'ant-eater' nose and the 'horn' positioned at the base of the engine air intake. Its aim was to increase downforce in the middle of the car and speed up the flow of air to the rear wing.

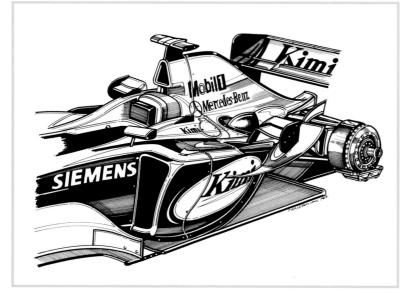

McLAREN MERCEDES MP4/20

The neat aerodynamics of the MP4/20, together with a revised cooling system (high-efficiency radiators inclined inside the sidepods) helped turn the McLaren into a rocket-ship. The same can be said for the FO110R, the 2005 Mercedes V10 engine that found the horsepower it had been lacking for many a year to make up for last year's disappointment. It was a pity for Ron Dennis' team that performance and reliability only arrived after the first few GPs, which was far too late to prevent Renault and Alonso from taking the world title. The marriage between the car and the Michelin tyres was also perfect, thanks to revised front and rear suspension, which were introduced from the San Marino GP onwards.

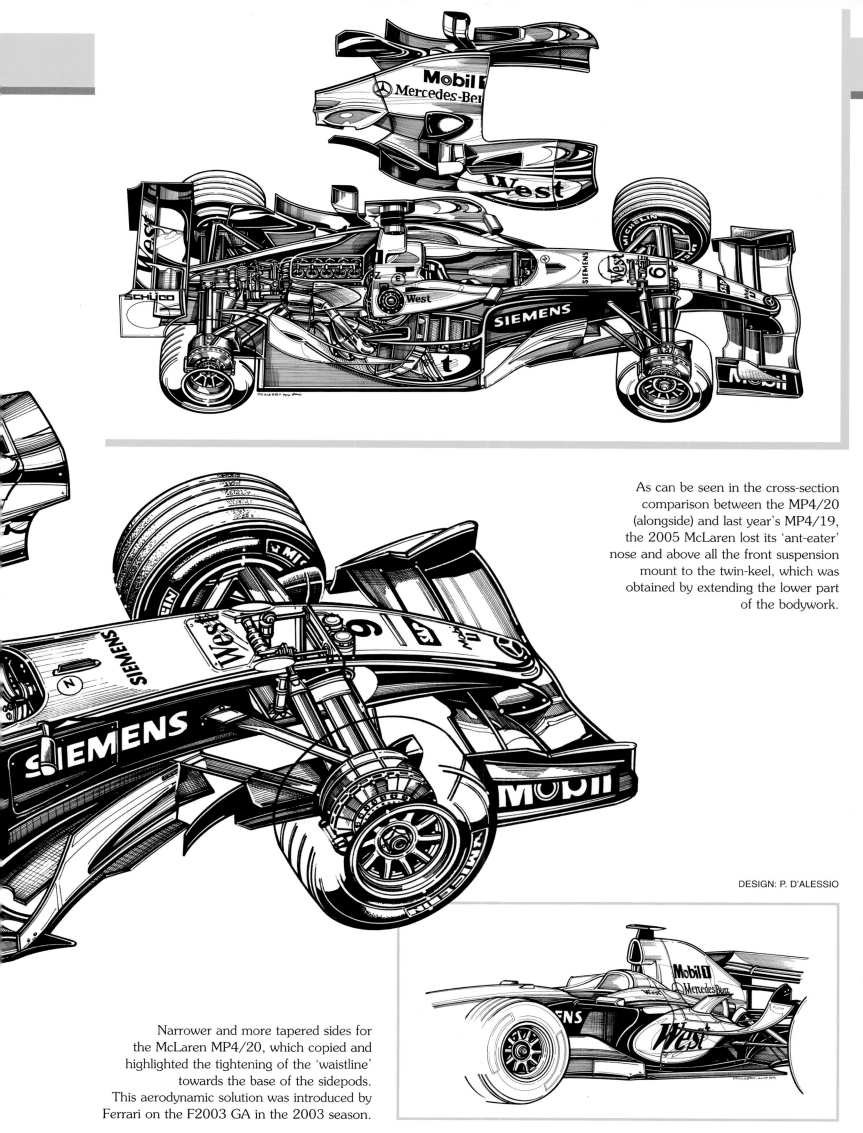

As can be seen in the cross-section comparison between the MP4/20 (alongside) and last year's MP4/19, the 2005 McLaren lost its 'ant-eater' nose and above all the front suspension mount to the twin-keel, which was obtained by extending the lower part of the bodywork.

DESIGN: P. D'ALESSIO

Narrower and more tapered sides for the McLaren MP4/20, which copied and highlighted the tightening of the 'waistline' towards the base of the sidepods. This aerodynamic solution was introduced by Ferrari on the F2003 GA in the 2003 season.

121

FERRARI F2005

After six world manufacturers' and five drivers' titles, at Maranello they probably decided to take a rain-check, but several non-technical factors, not necessarily dependent on the Prancing Horse team, were behind Ferrari's disastrous season. First, the F2004, transformed into the M version, with which Maranello tackled the early races of the season. Even though the results of the winter tests had not been particularly good, the Prancing Horse engineers hoped to resolve the situation because they were convinced that the most successful Ferrari of all time was still competitive and capable of at least fighting for the podium. The day after the Australian GP however it could be seen that the new technical regulations launched in 2005 had succeeded where McLaren and Williams had failed in the previous seasons, that is in knocking Ferrari off its throne. The Prancing Horse may have emerged unharmed by the rule change in 2001 which revolutionised the car's aerodynamics, and it also managed to overcome, albeit with some difficulty, the rule change imposing one engine for a race weekend as well as the crazy 2003 qualifying rules, but for the new 2005 norms it paid the price to the full. When the regulation changes were accompanied by the lack of suitable tyres for the new rules, either due to the Japanese constructor's conservative nature or because in 2004 Bridgestone had based development on tyres that performed much better over a short distance, then the picture gets worse and the consequences were plain for all to see. It would however not be fair to lay all the blame on Bridgestone. More realistically the responsibility for Ferrari's disastrous 2005 season is due to a series of circumstances, which included the Japanese tyres' technical shortcomings, and Maranello's decision over the past few seasons to increasingly opt for 'splendid isolation' in the preferential rapport with its Japanese partner. With the previous rules and throw-away tyres, everything worked perfectly, but with the need to use just one set of tyres, the situation now was different and the Ferrari pairing had changed from being the hare to the tortoise. To deal with this situation Ferrari, which last autumn had even suspected that it might be caught napping by the new regulations, should have speeded up the track launch of the F2005 and started the 2005 season with the new car. But this had not been possible because work on the F2005 began late and above all because at Maranello, after years of supremacy, radical changes were required that could not have been put into practice in just a few months. These changes resulted in the F2005, a car that in spite of the lack of results, was not actually that bad, otherwise Michael Schumacher would not have been able to have such fantastic races as the San Marino or the Hungarian GP, where he was almost a second quicker than his rivals in qualifying. The other side of the coin was represented by the Turkish and the Italian GPs, where the seven-times world champion and Rubens Barrichello, in clear tyre difficulty, were almost two seconds a lap slower than the opposition. How can these ups and downs in performance be explained? In 2005 Ferrari built a more conservative car than McLaren and Renault, but above all it was a model that only under certain conditions was able to repeat on the track the excellent results it had obtained in the wind-tunnel or during race simulations. In this aspect the 2005 Ferrari was similar to the unsuccessful F92A car of 1992, which on paper should have annihilated the opposition but which turned out to be a total fiasco. The future of Ferrari however is not as bleak as what it has been over the past few months. Although it is true that Renault and McLaren are currently the cars to beat, several technical innovations introduced by Ferrari this year such as the narrow transmission and the smaller radiant masses, should allow for a margin of improvement for the red cars, once the new eight-cylinder 2.4 litre engine is up and running.

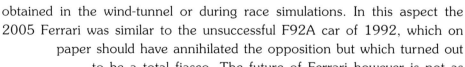

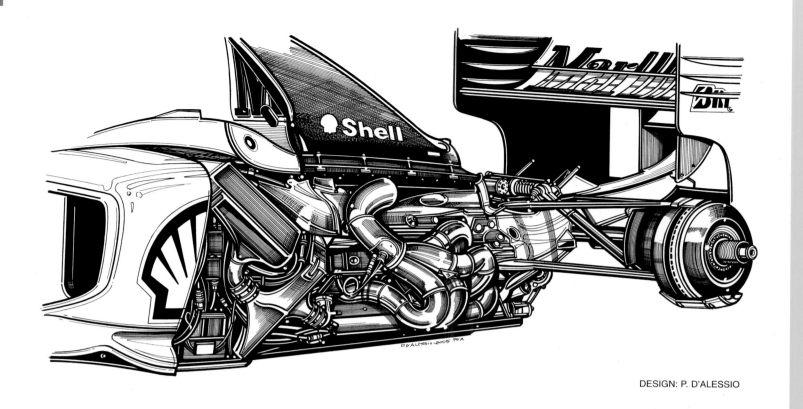

To increase rear tapering, the Ferrari F2005 was fitted with a neat, new-generation gearbox. This was a lot smaller and housed several accessories and the suspension mounting points, as well as the new Sachs rotational dampers. To reduce the size of the transversal gearbox, Ferrari engineers also literally turned the exhaust outlets round, thus freeing the area next to the gearbox. This modification eliminated the need for the periscope style exhausts (see design above), which for several years had characterized all Ferrari's Formula 1 cars. Below, the F2005's new wings.

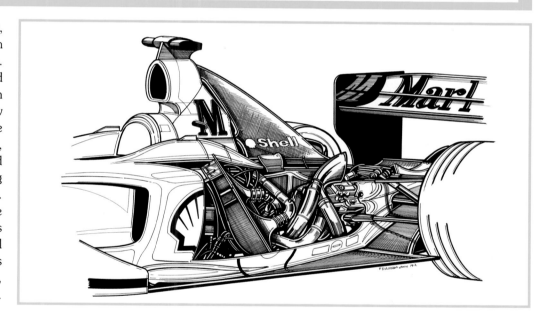

FERRARI F2005

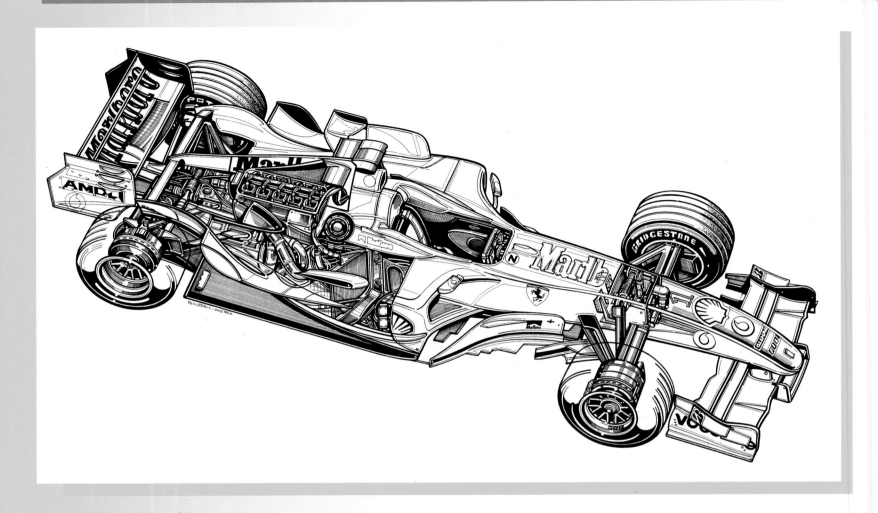

DESIGN: P. D'ALESSIO

The F2005 (see alongside) represented a considerable step forward over the unsuccessful F2004 M (see above) which was used in the first few GPs of 2005. Even though the shape was not that dissimilar to last year's car, there were several major differences. The nose for example had a lower profile in the middle to gain downforce. The upper part of the chassis is dug out, while the sides are smaller and more compact than the previous version. The real leap in quality over the F2004 however was hidden beneath the bodywork. The F2005 has different internal fluid dynamics, as well as different radiators, while the exhaust outlets were turned around and moved forward. The 055 engine was new, but still as reliable as ever, despite not being as powerful as the Mercedes or Toyota V10.

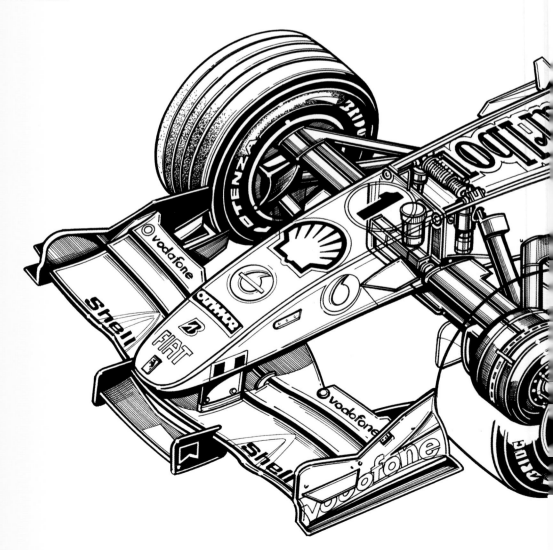

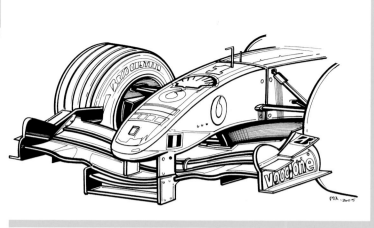

The central box front wing on the nose of the F2005,
with its additional upper profile, was not much of a success.
In 2005 Ferrari paid the price for the defection
by aerodynamics engineer Nick Tombazis,
the father of the F2001, F2002
and F2003 GA, to McLaren.

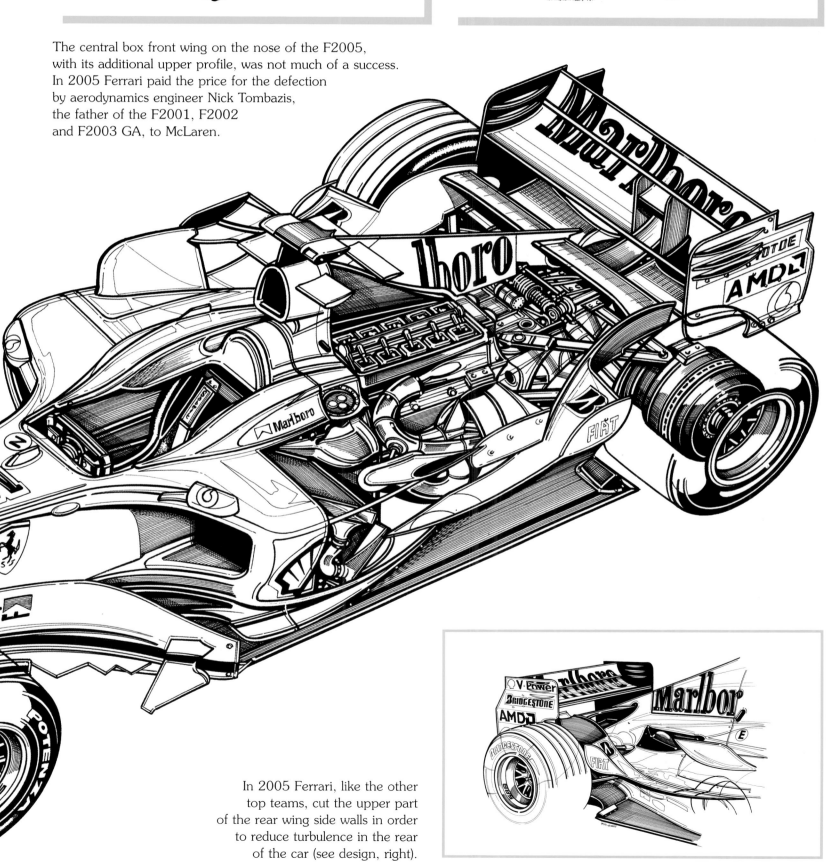

In 2005 Ferrari, like the other
top teams, cut the upper part
of the rear wing side walls in order
to reduce turbulence in the rear
of the car (see design, right).

BAR-HONDA, RED BULL

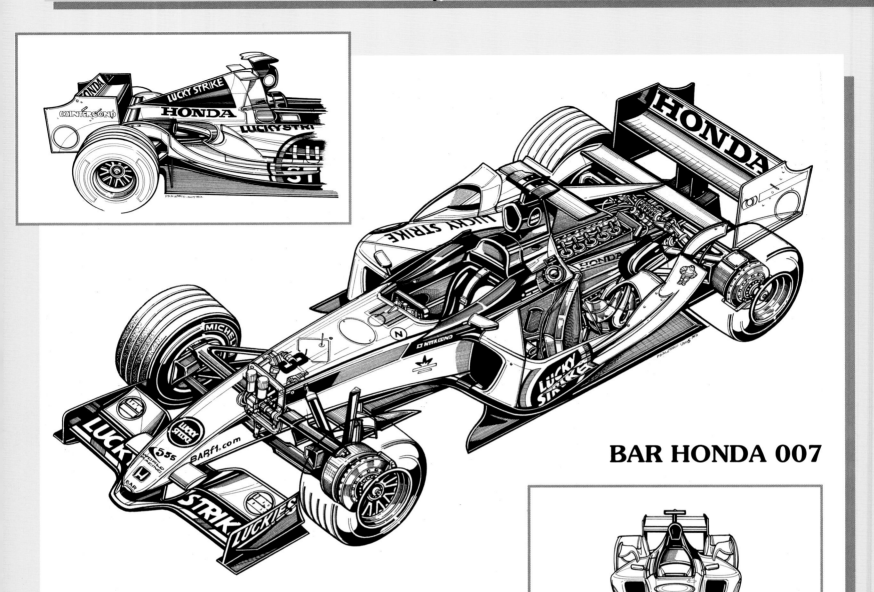

BAR HONDA 007

After being disqualified at Imola, the BAR-Honda 007 (see cross-section above, see right the original front wing with its central 'beak' shape) began a slow but constant return to the top positions, where the Anglo-Japanese team last year could be seen regularly. Still with Japan, the Toyota TF105 (see above right) also produced some excellent performances. Mike Gascoyne, the engineer lured away from Renault at a price, made his presence felt and the testing skills of a driver of the calibre of Jarno Trulli allowed the Japanese manufacturer to gain a foothold amongst the top teams. The word in the paddock is that the Toyota ten-cylinder engine was the most powerful on the grid, together with the V10 Mercedes.

RED BULL

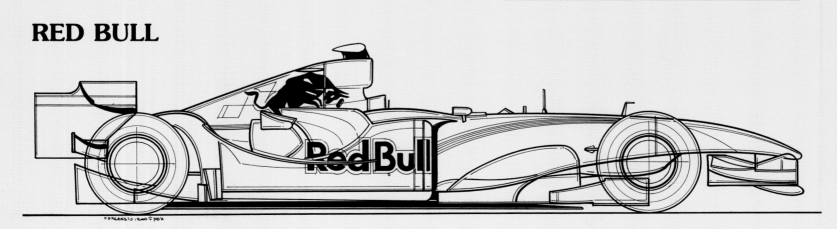

TOYOTA, WILLIAMS BMW

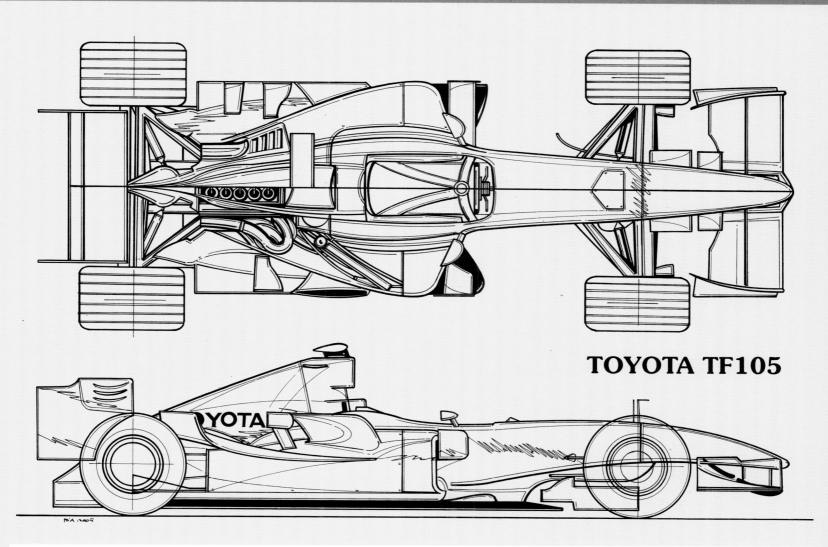

TOYOTA TF105

DESIGN: P. D'ALESSIO

The 2005 season saw numerous ups and downs in the performance rating of certain teams. One on the way up was undoubtedly Red Bull, the former Jaguar outfit (see lower left), which in 2006 will have the 2.4 litre Ferrari V8 engine. Williams (see below), which went in the opposite direction, lost the support of BMW and next year will be forced to race with eight-cylinder Cosworth engines.

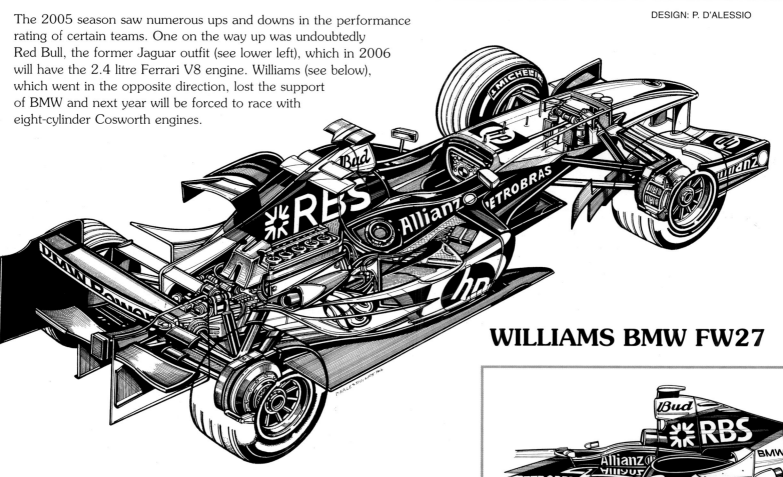

WILLIAMS BMW FW27

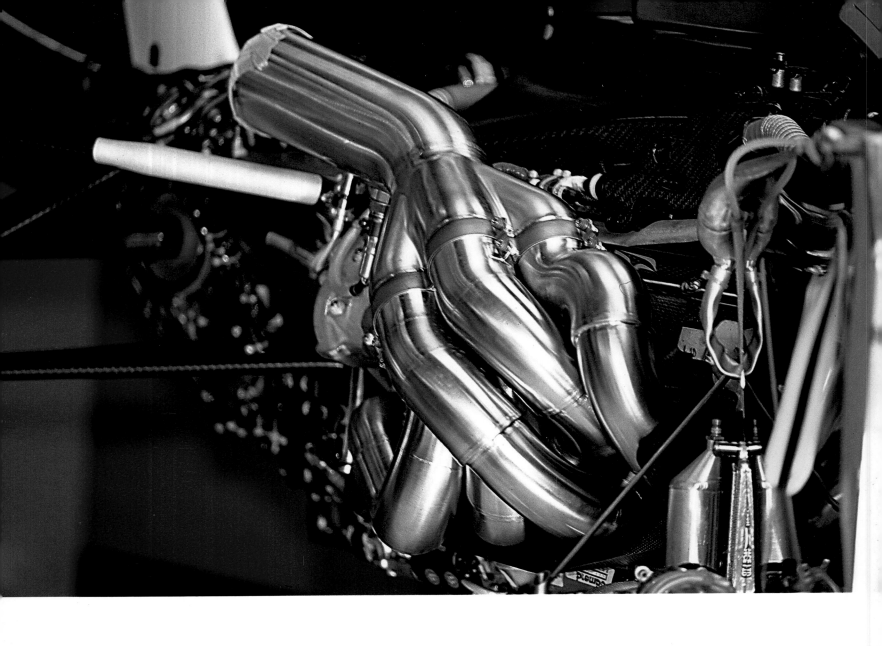

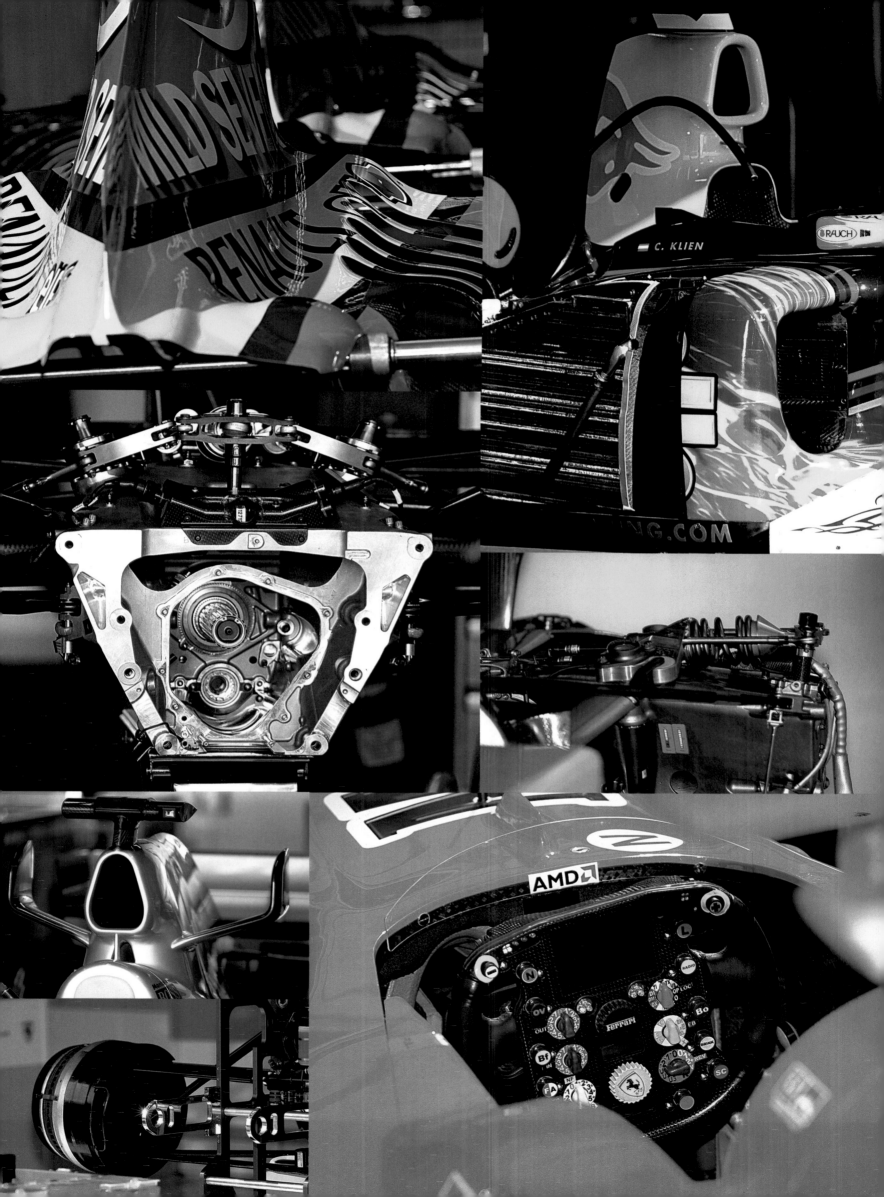

POLE POSITION

'90	A. Senna	'98	M. Hakkinen
'91	A. Senna	'99	M. Hakkinen
'92	N. Mansell	'00	M. Hakkinen
'93	A. Senna	'01	M. Schumacher
'94	N. Mansell	'02	R. Barrichello
'95	D. Hill	'03	M. Schumacher
'96	J. Villeneuve	'04	M. Schumacher
'97	J. Villeneuve	'05	G. Fisichella

	1°	2°	3°
'90	N. Piquet	N. Mansell	A. Prost
'91	A. Senna	N. Mansell	G. Berger
'92	G. Berger	M. Schumacher	M. Brundle
'93	A. Senna	A. Prost	D. Hill
'94	N. Mansell	G. Berger	M. Brundle
'95	D. Hill	O. Panis	G. Morbidelli
'96	D. Hill	J. Villeneuve	E. Irvine
'97	D. Coulthard	M. Schumacher	M. Hakkinen
'98	M. Hakkinen	D. Coulthard	H.H. Frentzen
'99	E. Irvine	H.H. Frentzen	R. Schumacher
'00	M. Schumacher	R. Barrichello	R. Schumacher
'01	M. Schumacher	D. Coulthard	R. Barrichello
'02	M. Schumacher	J.P. Montoya	K. Raikkonen
'03	D. Coulthard	J.P. Montoya	K. Raikkonen
'04	M. Schumacher	R. Barrichello	F. Alonso

STARTING GRID

1
 GIANCARLO FISICHELLA RENAULT
 JARNO TRULLI TOYOTA

2
 MARK WEBBER WILLIAMS
 JACQUES VILLENEUVE SAUBER

3
 DAVID COULTHARD RED BULL
 CHRISTIAN KLIEN RED BULL

4
 NICK HEIDFELD WILLIAMS
 JENSON BUTTON BAR

5
 JUAN PABLO MONTOYA MCLAREN
 KIMI RAIKKONEN MCLAREN

6
 RUBENS BARRICHELLO FERRARI
 NARAIN KARTHIKEYAN JORDAN

7
 FERNANDO ALONSO RENAULT
 TIAGO MONTEIRO JORDAN

8
 RALF SCHUMACHER TOYOTA
 PATRICK FRIESACHER MINARDI

9
 CHRISTIJAN ALBERS MINARDI
 FELIPE MASSA SAUBER

10
 MICHAEL SCHUMACHER FERRARI
 TAKUMA SATO BAR

RESULTS

	DRIVER	CAR	KPH	GAP
1	G. Fisichella	Renault	215,168	-
2	R. Barrichello	Ferrari	214,932	0'05"553
3	F. Alonso	Renault	214,883	0'06"712
4	D. Coulthard	Red Bull	214,484	0'16"131
5	M. Webber	Williams	214,451	0'16"908
6	J.P. Montoya	McLaren	213,687	0'35"033
7	C. Klien	Red Bull	213,521	0'38"997
8	K. Raikkonen	McLaren	213,495	0'39"633
9	J. Trulli	Toyota	212,516	1'03"108
10	F. Massa	Sauber	212,463	1'04"393
11	J. Button	BAR	212,107	Retired
12	R. Schumacher	Toyota	211,287	1 lap
13	J. Villeneuve	Sauber	210,557	1 lap
14	T. Sato	BAR	210,885	Retired
15	N. Karthikeian	Jordan	207,549	2 laps
16	T. Monteiro	Jordan	205,364	2 laps
17	P. Friesacher	Minardi	198,393	4 laps

RETIREMENTS

M. Schumacher	Ferrari	42	Accident
N. Heidfeld	Williams	42	Accident
C. Albers	Minardi	16	Gearbox

THE RACE

DRIVER	CAR	LAP	FASTEST LAP	TOP SPEED
F. Alonso	Renault	24	1'25"683	320,7
G. Fisichella	Renault	55	1'25"994	319,0
R. Barrichello	Ferrari	54	1'26"233	319,5
K. Raikkonen	McLaren	55	1'26"255	318,7
J. Button	BAR	55	1'26"260	314,5
M. Schumacher	Ferrari	38	1'26"261	322,7
J.P. Montoya	McLaren	41	1'26"393	315,3
M. Webber	Williams	37	1'26"493	316,6
R. Schumacher	Toyota	56	1'26"536	313,9
C. Klien	Red Bull	39	1'26"627	317,3
D. Coulthard	Red Bull	40	1'26"690	317,8
N. Heidfeld	Williams	38	1'26"854	316,7
F. Massa	Sauber	55	1'26"893	320,3
J. Trulli	Toyota	56	1'27"116	312,6
J. Villeneuve	Sauber	54	1'27"745	316,0
T. Sato	BAR	36	1'27"877	319,0
N. Karthikeian	Jordan	36	1'27"970	314,7
T. Monteiro	Jordan	16	1'28"999	313,9
P. Friesacher	Minardi	22	1'32"852	310,7
C. Albers	Minardi	11	1'33"144	302,4

AUSTRALIAN GP

THE RETURN OF FISICHELLA

The Renaults were quick to confirm on the Albert Park circuit
that their positive winter testing performances had not been a fluke.
But the Renaults were not the only cars that stood out in qualifying.
Toyota were on the front row with Jarno Trulli, Sauber on row 2 with
Villeneuve and Red Bull one row behind with David Coulthard.
Ferrari started off badly with Barrichello setting eleventh quickest time
and Schumacher lining up on the final row of the grid alongside Sato after both
had to change engines during practice. The grid positions were a bit misleading
however as qualifying had been affected by the rain that fell on Saturday in
the first session, but Fisichella, Trulli and Coulthard had proved to be quick
in any case in any track conditions.
At the start Fisichella powered into the lead and conducted the race with
the skill of a consummate champion, preserving his tyres and engine and keeping
one eye on his closest rivals. First Trulli tried to attack his fellow Italian, then it was
the turn of Coulthard and finally Barrichello, who had made a superb recovery
from eleventh on the grid. Trulli, who had started the race with a low fuel load,
trailed Fisichella for 17 laps but then had to make a pit stop and his Toyota
began to have a few handling problems which dropped him down to ninth.
Coulthard on the other hand, maybe galvanized by a points bonus contract
with Red Bull, seemed totally rejuvenated and held second place until lap 41.
Then came his pit stop and he dropped down to fourth, a bitter
disappointment for the Scottish driver in his 176th GP.
Meanwhile Barrichello was in superb form and was making up place after place.
The Brazilian went on to finish second, scoring a podium place for Ferrari.
Alonso, who started thirteenth, was also scything his way through the field
and the Spaniard could have grabbed second from Barrichello at the end
but was slowed by Villeneuve and had to settle for third place and points
in the Constructors' standings.
It was a black day for the world champion. Schumacher started from the final
row of the grid but collided with Nick Heidfeld on lap 43 and had to retire.

HIGHLIGHTS

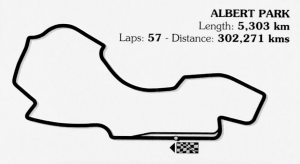

34-year-old David Coulthard, with 175 GPs,
13 wins and 12 pole positions to his name,
finished a superb fourth after holding on to the
runner-up slot for two-thirds of the race.
It was a surprising result for Red Bull seeing
as the car is virtually the same one as the disastrous
2004 Jaguar. It is also worth mentioning that
the second Red Bull, driven by Austrian Klien,
also scored points in seventh place.

Gentlemen, start your engines! It's time
for another season behind the wheel, surrounded
by the usual array of beautiful women, young
up-and-coming drivers and a series of regulation
changes that will make this year's championship
battle more wide open than ever.

CHAMPIONSHIPS POINTS		AUSTRALIAN GP	MALAYSIAN GP	BAHRAIN GP	SAN MARINO GP	SPANISH GP	MONACO GP	EUROPEAN GP	CANADIAN GP	UNITED STATES GP	FRENCH GP	BRITISH GP	GERMAN GP	HUNGARIAN GP	TURKISH GP	ITALIAN GP	BELGIUM GP	BRAZILIAN GP	JAPANESE GP	CHINA GP	TOTAL POINT
1	G. FISICHELLA	10																			10
2	R. BARRICHELLO	8																			8
3	F. ALONSO	6																			6
4	D. COULTHARD	5																			5
5	M. WEBBER	4																			4
6	J.P. MONTOYA	3																			3
7	C. KLIEN	2																			2
8	K. RAIKKONEN	1																			1
9	J. TRULLI	-																			0
10	F. MASSA	-																			0
11	J. BUTTON	-																			0
12	R. SCHUMACHER	-																			0
13	J. VILLENEUVE	-																			0
14	T. SATO	-																			0
15	N. KARTHIKEYAN	-																			0
16	T. MONTEIRO	-																			0
17	P. FRIESACHER	-																			0
18	M. SCHUMACHER	-																			0
19	N. HEIDFELD	-																			0
20	C. ALBERS	-																			0

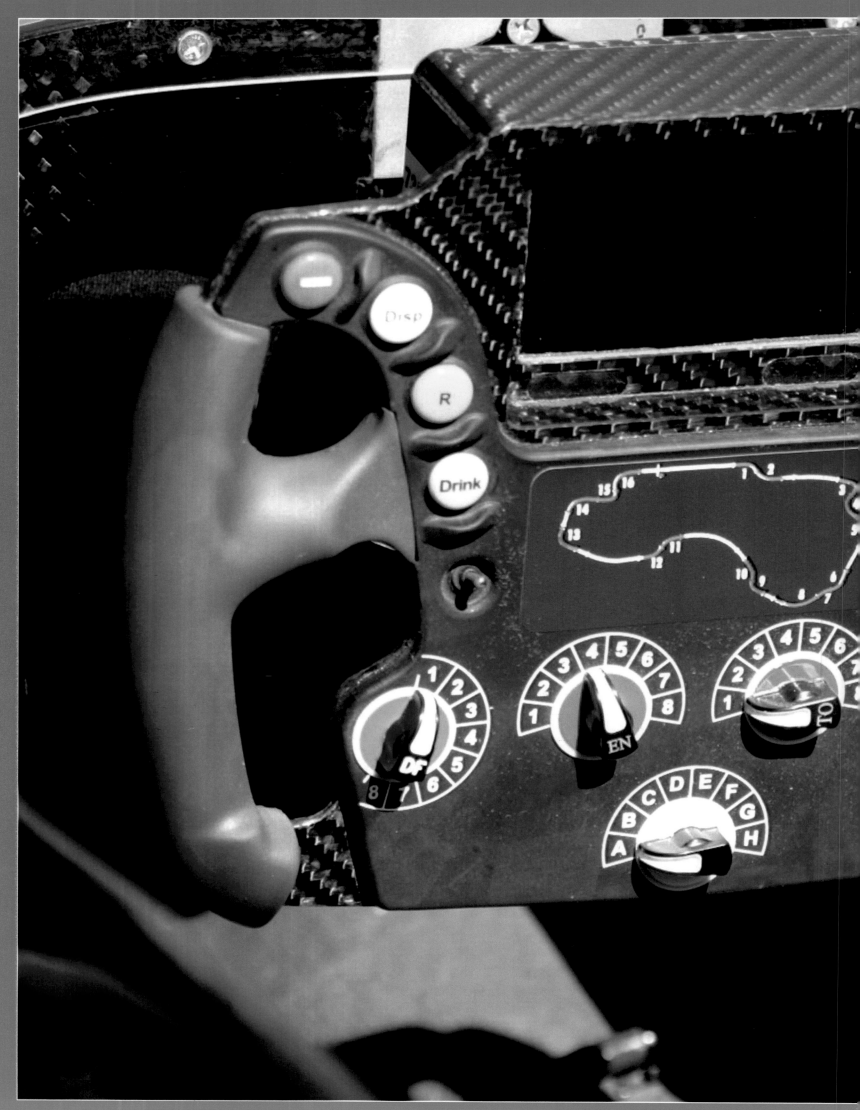

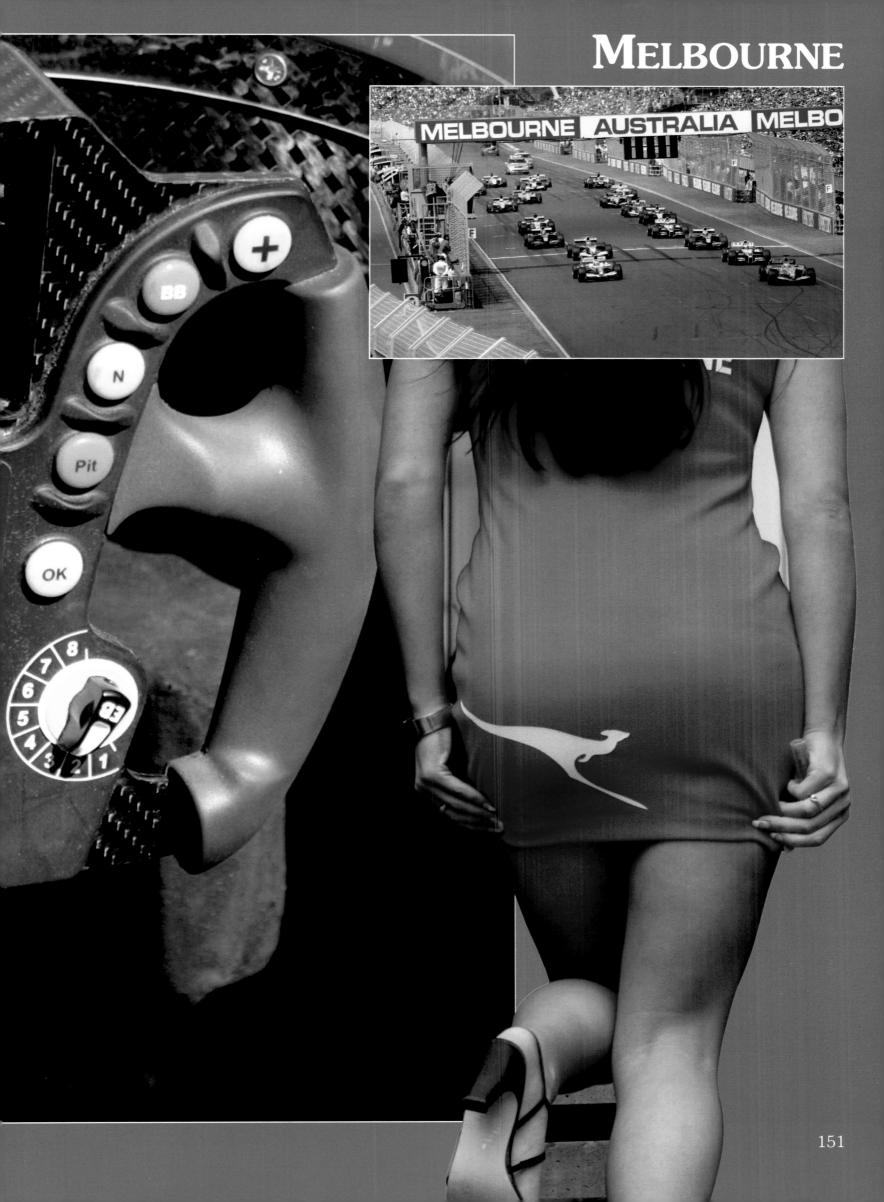

SEPANG
20 MARCH 2005

POLE POSITION

'90	-	'98	-
'91	-	'99	M. Schumacher
'92	-	'00	M. Schumacher
'93	-	'01	M. Schumacher
'94	-	'02	M. Schumacher
'95	-	'03	F. Alonso
'96	-	'04	M. Schumacher
'97	-	'05	F. Alonso

STARTING GRID

Pos		
1	**FERNANDO ALONSO** RENAULT	**JARNO TRULLI** TOYOTA
2	**GIANCARLO FISICHELLA** RENAULT	**MARK WEBBER** WILLIAMS
3	**RALF SCHUMACHER** TOYOTA	**KIMI RAIKKONEN** McLAREN
4	**CHRISTIAN KLIEN** RED BULL	**DAVID COULTHARD** RED BULL
5	**JENSON BUTTON** BAR	**NICK HEIDFELD** WILLIAMS
6	**JUAN PABLO MONTOYA** McLAREN	**RUBENS BARRICHELLO** FERRARI
7	**MICHAEL SCHUMACHER** FERRARI	**FELIPE MASSA** SAUBER
8	**ANTHONY DAVIDSON** BAR	**JACQUES VILLENEUVE** SAUBER
9	**NARAIN KARTHIKEYAN** JORDAN	**TIAGO MONTEIRO** JORDAN
10	**CHRISTIJAN ALBERS** MINARDI	**PATRICK FRIESACHER** MINARDI

	1°	2°	3°
'90	-	-	-
'91	-	-	-
'92	-	-	-
'93	-	-	-
'94	-	-	-
'95	-	-	-
'96	-	-	-
'97	-	-	-
'98	-	-	-
'99	M. Hakkinen	M. Schumacher	E. Irvine
'00	M. Schumacher	D. Coulthard	R. Barrichello
'01	M. Schumacher	R. Barrichello	D. Coulthard
'02	R. Schumacher	J.P. Montoya	M. Schumacher
'03	K. Raikkonen	R. Barrichello	F. Alonso
'04	M. Schumacher	J.P. Montoya	J. Button

RESULTS

	DRIVER	CAR	KPH	GAP
1	F. Alonso	Renault	203,407	-
2	J. Trulli	Toyota	202,511	0'24"327
3	N. Heidfeld	Williams	202,222	0'32"188
4	J.P. Montoya	McLaren	201,877	0'41"631
5	R. Schumacher	Toyota	201,505	0'51"854
6	D. Coulthard	Red Bull	200,756	1'12"543
7	M. Schumacher	Ferrari	200,488	1'19"988
8	C. Klien	Red Bull	200,458	1'20"835
9	K. Raikkonen	McLaren	200,431	1'21"580
10	F. Massa	Sauber	199,351	1 lap
11	N. Karthikeyan	Jordan	197,275	2 laps
12	T. Monteiro	Jordan	191,871	3 laps
13	C. Albers	Minardi	187,718	4 laps

RETIREMENTS

R. Barrichello	Ferrari	49	Handling problem
G. Fisichella	Renault	36	Accident
M. Webber	Williams	36	Accident
J. Villeneuve	Sauber	26	Spin
J. Button	BAR	2	Engine
A. Davidson	BAR	2	Engine
P. Friesacher	Minardi	2	Spin

THE RACE

DRIVER	CAR	LAP	FASTEST LAP	TOP SPEED
K. Raikkonen	McLaren	23	1'35"483	309,3
N. Heidfeld	Williams	40	1'35"712	311,8
J. Trulli	Toyota	18	1'35"816	310,0
F. Alonso	Renault	18	1'35"899	312,7
M. Webber	Williams	20	1'36"026	306,1
G. Fisichella	Renault	21	1'36"182	314,2
R. Schumacher	Toyota	15	1'36"321	312,4
J.P. Montoya	McLaren	42	1'36"585	307,4
D. Coulthard	Red Bull	18	1'36"790	309,1
R. Barrichello	Ferrari	22	1'36"878	314,5
C. Klien	Red Bull	17	1'36"902	316,2
M. Schumacher	Ferrari	41	1'36"982	316,6
F. Massa	Sauber	18	1'37"212	312,0
J. Button	BAR	2	1'37"912	308,8
J. Villeneuve	Sauber	18	1'38"058	309,4
N. Karthikeyan	Jordan	18	1'39"833	312,2
T. Monteiro	Jordan	36	1'40"432	307,9
A. Davidson	BAR	2	1'41"470	305,3
C. Albers	Minardi	12	1'42"465	305,3
P. Friesacher	Minardi	2	1'43"558	311,0

MALAYSIAN GP

SEPANG
Length: **5,543 km**
Laps: **56** - Distance: **310,408 kms**

RENAULT AGAIN!

Pole position and a win for Fisichella in Australia; pole position and a win
for Alonso two weeks later in Sepang, in a race that was dominated by stifling
oppressive heat that created major tyre problems for Ferrari as well as
McLaren on a tarmac where the temperature reached over 50 degrees.
Apart from Alonso, qualifying threw up excellent performances
from Fisichella in third and the two surprising Toyotas of Trulli in second
and Ralf Schumacher in fifth.
It was another qualifying session to forget for Ferrari, with Rubens Barrichello
and Michael Schumacher lining up twelfth and thirteenth on the grid respectively
while Anthony Davidson replaced the still unfit Sato in the second BAR.
Alonso made his usual superb start and immediately opened up a small gap on
the rest of the field, followed by Trulli in the Toyota and his team-mate Fisichella.
The race was turning into a monologue, with the young Spanish driver
easily controlling his rivals, slipping in a few quick laps now and again just
to show the rest who was boss.
Team-mate Fisichella however found that his Renault was far
from perfect and the Italian was struggling to keep hold of his third place.
First he ran over the kerb, ruining his aerodynamic tweaks, and then
he destroyed it completely on lap 37 when he spun in front of Webber
in the Williams, putting both drivers out of the race.
Raikkonen was unfortunate in that he had a high-speed tyre failure on the
start-finish straight that forced him to complete an entire lap on three wheels.
The Finn eventually finished ninth after setting the fastest lap, but would surely
have finished on the podium had he not been forced to stop to change the tyre.
The final podium slot went to Heidfeld in the Williams, after team-mate
Webber and Fisichella, who were both ahead of him, had to retire.
After their disastrous qualifying, things went just as bad for Ferrari in the race.
Barichello was lapped by Klien in the Red Bull and then had to retire with a
handling imbalance caused by a piece of rubber jammed into the rear wing.

The 30-year-old Italian, Jarno Trulli, who has taken
part in 128 GPs, winning one at Montecarlo in 2004,
finally took the Toyota to its first podium finish
after three years in F1.
A major part in this result must be attributed
to the set-up work done during the winter tests
by the Italian driver, who has always been quicker
than team-mate Ralf Schumacher both in qualifying
and in the races.

After Fisichella's triumph in Australia
with the Renault, once again it was the French
car that took the maximum points, this time
with emerging talent Fernando Alonso.

CHAMPIONSHIPS POINTS		AUSTRALIAN GP	MALAYSIAN GP	BAHRAIN GP	SAN MARINO GP	SPANISH GP	MONACO GP	EUROPEAN GP	CANADIAN GP	UNITED STATES GP	FRENCH GP	BRITISH GP	GERMAN GP	HUNGARIAN GP	TURKISH GP	ITALIAN GP	BELGIUM GP	BRAZILIAN GP	JAPANESE GP	CHINA GP	TOTAL POINT
1	F. ALONSO	6	10																		16
2	G. FISICHELLA	10	-																		10
3	J. TRULLI	-	8																		8
4	R. BARRICHELLO	8	-																		8
5	J.P. MONTOYA	3	5																		8
6	D. COULTHARD	5	3																		8
7	N. HEIDFELD	-	6																		6
8	R. SCHUMACHER	-	4																		4
9	M. WEBBER	4	-																		4
10	C. KLIEN	2	1																		3
11	M. SCHUMACHER	-	2																		2
12	K. RAIKKONEN	1	-																		1
13	F. MASSA	-	-																		0
14	J. BUTTON	-	-																		0
15	J. VILLENEUVE	-	-																		0
16	T. SATO	-	-																		0
17	N. KARTHIKEYAN	-	-																		0
18	T. MONTEIRO	-	-																		0
19	P. FRIESACHER	-	-																		0
20	C. ALBERS	-	-																		0
21	A. DAVIDSON	/	-																		0

POLE POSITION

'90	-	'98	-
'91	-	'99	-
'92	-	'00	-
'93	-	'01	-
'94	-	'02	-
'95	-	'03	-
'96	-	'04	M. Schumacher
'97	-	'05	F. Alonso

STARTING GRID

1 FERNANDO ALONSO — RENAULT | MICHAEL SCHUMACHER — FERRARI

2 JARNO TRULLI — TOYOTA | NICK HEIDFELD — WILLIAMS

3 MARK WEBBER — WILLIAMS | RALF SCHUMACHER — TOYOTA

4 CHRISTIAN KLIEN — RED BULL | PEDRO DE LA ROSA — MCLAREN

5 KIMI RAIKKONEN — MCLAREN | GIANCARLO FISICHELLA — RENAULT

6 JENSON BUTTON — BAR | FELIPE MASSA — SAUBER

7 TAKUMA SATO — BAR | DAVID COULTHARD — RED BULL

8 JACQUES VILLENEUVE — SAUBER | TIAGO MONTEIRO — JORDAN

9 NARAIN KARTHIKEYAN — JORDAN | CHRISTIJAN ALBERS — MINARDI

10 PATRICK FRIESACHER — MINARDI | RUBENS BARRICHELLO — FERRARI

	1°	2°	3°
'04	M. Schumacher	R. Barrichello	J. Button

RESULTS

	DRIVER	CAR	KPH	GAP
1	F. Alonso	Renault	207,082	-
2	J. Trulli	Toyota	206,565	0'13"409
3	K. Raikkonen	McLaren	205,850	0'32"063
4	R. Schumacher	Toyota	205,043	0'53"272
5	P. De La Rosa	McLaren	204,600	1'04"988
6	M. Webber	Williams	204,235	1'14"701
7	F. Massa	Sauber	203,360	1 lap
8	D. Coulthard	Red Bull	202,910	1 lap
9	R. Barrichello	Ferrari	202,638	1 lap
10	T. Monteiro	Jordan	196,528	2 laps
11	P. Friesacher	Minardi	192,931	3 laps
12	C. Albers	Minardi	192,477	4 laps

RETIREMENTS

J. Villeneuve	Sauber	54	Accident
J. Button	BAR	46	Clutch
T. Sato	BAR	27	Brakes
N. Heidfeld	Williams	25	Engine
M. Schumacher	Ferrari	12	Hydraulic circuit
G. Fisichella	Renault	4	Engine
N. Karthikeyan	Jordan	2	Electrical
C. Klien	Red Bull	0	Electrical

THE RACE

DRIVER	CAR	LAP	FASTEST LAP	TOP SPEED
P. De La Rosa	McLaren	43	1'31"447	337,7
F. Alonso	Renault	39	1'31"713	329,5
K. Raikkonen	McLaren	41	1'31"822	333,0
J. Trulli	Toyota	41	1'32"324	326,2
J. Button	BAR	45	1'32"411	323,1
R. Schumacher	Toyota	36	1'32"683	326,2
M. Schumacher	Ferrari	7	1'32"886	332,9
R. Barrichello	Ferrari	23	1'32"976	328,6
N. Heidfeld	Williams	19	1'33"055	323,8
M. Webber	Williams	20	1'33"087	325,9
T. Sato	BAR	23	1'33"124	325,9
F. Massa	Sauber	40	1'33"326	330,1
D. Coulthard	Red Bull	42	1'33"417	331,1
J. Villeneuve	Sauber	24	1'33"458	327,5
T. Monteiro	Jordan	18	1'35"744	326,8
P. Friesacher	Minardi	16	1'36"432	322,9
C. Albers	Minardi	3	1'36"913	320,1
G. Fisichella	Renault	2	1'37"036	318,0
N. Karthikeyan	Jordan	2	1'37"533	288,2
C. Klien	Red Bull	-	-	-

BAHRAIN GP

BAHRAIN
Length:
5,412 km
Laps: **57**
Distance:
308,238 kms

ALONSO REPEATS SEPANG SUCCESS

After just three GPs, the young Spanish driver is already
the most likely candidate for the 2005 Drivers' title. Alonso again set pole,
almost half-a-second ahead of Michael Schumacher with the new F2005
and the German was followed by Jarno Trulli, who was continuing
his good performance with the Toyota.

The last driver on the grid was Rubens Barrichello, who had to change
his engine during practice. Montoya, who had injured a shoulder playing tennis,
was absent in Bahrain and his place was taken by a superlative De La Rosa,
who was not only quicker than Raikkonen in qualifying, but would also go
on to take an excellent fifth place in the race, together with the fastest lap.

At the lights Alonso powered away, followed by Schummy, Trulli and Webber,
while Barrichello had already made up five places during the opening lap.
Schumacher's race with the brand-new Ferrari F2005 didn't last long
as the German rolled to a halt out on the circuit on lap 12 with hydraulic failure.
Before that, both Fisichella and Karthikeyan (Jordan) had to retire,
while Klien didn't even manage to start following an electrical problem.

Up at the front Alonso was easily controlling the race and further down the field
Barrichello moved into seventh position ten laps from the flag, but then his tyres
started to go off. Felipe Massa caught him and so did Coulthard, and the
Brazilian dropped to ninth place at the finish after being lapped.

Alonso went on to clinch another win in Bahrain, followed by Trulli
and Raikkonen. The Finn had a disappointing weekend after making a
few mistakes both in qualifying and the race.

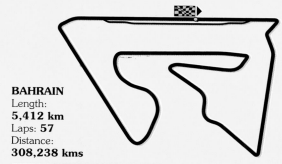

HIGHLIGHTS

It cannot be easy for a driver, after a two-year break,
to return to GPs and find the determination necessary to
compete with the best. But obviously no one had told
Pedro De La Rosa, who put together one of his best ever
performances right from the start of the weekend,
the Brazilian even outpacing team-mate Raikkonen.
It was a pity he got caught up in the fighting mid-field
group with Webber, Barrichello and Button, because he
had one of the quickest cars out there, but as we all know,
overtaking in modern-day F1 is not easy.

PHOTO PORTFOLIO

Alonso was again the winner in Bahrain,
with Trulli taking his first podium of the season
for Toyota. Montoya was missing from the grid
after injuring his shoulder playing tennis.

CHAMPIONSHIPS POINTS		AUSTRALIAN GP	MALAYSIAN GP	BAHRAIN GP	SAN MARINO GP	SPANISH GP	MONACO GP	EUROPEAN GP	CANADIAN GP	UNITED STATES GP	FRENCH GP	BRITISH GP	GERMAN GP	HUNGARIAN GP	TURKISH GP	ITALIAN GP	BELGIUM GP	BRAZILIAN GP	JAPANESE GP	CHINA GP	TOTAL POINT
1	F. ALONSO	6	10	10																	26
2	J. TRULLI	-	8	8																	16
3	G. FISICHELLA	10	-	-																	10
4	R. SCHUMACHER	-	4	5																	9
5	D. COULTHARD	5	3	1																	9
6	R. BARRICHELLO	8	-	-																	8
7	J.P. MONTOYA	3	5	/																	8
8	K. RAIKKONEN	1	-	6																	7
9	M. WEBBER	4	-	3																	7
10	N. HEIDFELD	-	6	-																	6
11	P. DE LA ROSA	/	/	4																	4
12	C. KLIEN	2	1	-																	3
13	F. MASSA	-	-	2																	2
14	M. SCHUMACHER	-	2	-																	2
15	T. MONTEIRO	-	-	-																	0
16	J. BUTTON	-	-	-																	0
17	J. VILLENEUVE	-	-	-																	0
18	T. SATO	-	-	-																	0
19	N. KARTHIKEYAN	-	-	-																	0
20	P. FRIESACHER	-	-	-																	0
21	C. ALBERS	-	-	-																	0
22	A. DAVIDSON	/	-	/																	0

Pole Position

'90	A. Senna	'98	D. Coulthard
'91	A. Senna	'99	M. Hakkinen
'92	N. Mansell	'00	M. Hakkinen
'93	A. Prost	'01	D. Coulthard
'94	A. Senna	'02	M. Schumacher
'95	M. Schumacher	'03	M. Schumacher
'96	M. Schumacher	'04	J. Button
'97	J. Villeneuve	'05	K. Raikkonen

Starting Grid

1	**KIMI RAIKKONEN** McLAREN	**FERNANDO ALONSO** RENAULT	
2	**JENSON BUTTON** BAR	**MARK WEBBER** WILLIAMS	
3	**JARNO TRULLI** TOYOTA	**TAKUMA SATO** BAR	
4	**ALEXANDER WURZ** McLAREN	**NICK HEIDFELD** WILLIAMS	
5	**RUBENS BARRICHELLO** FERRARI	**RALF SCHUMACHER** TOYOTA	
6	**JACQUES VILLENEUVE** SAUBER	**GIANCARLO FISICHELLA** RENAULT	
7	**MICHAEL SCHUMACHER** FERRARI	**DAVID COULTHARD** RED BULL	
8	**VITANTONIO LIUZZI** RED BULL	**NARAIN KARTHIKEYAN** JORDAN	
9	**TIAGO MONTEIRO** JORDAN	**FELIPE MASSA** SAUBER	
10	**PATRICK FRIESACHER** MINARDI	**CHRISTIJAN ALBERS** MINARDI	

	1°	2°	3°
'90	R. Patrese	G. Berger	A. Nannini
'91	A. Senna	G. Berger	J. Lehto
'92	N. Mansell	R. Patrese	A. Senna
'93	A. Prost	M. Schumacher	M. Brundle
'94	M. Schumacher	N. Larini	M. Hakkinen
'95	D. Hill	J. Alesi	G. Berger
'96	D. Hill	M. Schumacher	G. Berger
'97	H.H. Frentzen	M. Schumacher	E. Irvine
'98	D. Coulthard	M. Schumacher	E. Irvine
'99	M. Schumacher	D. Coulthard	R. Barrichello
'00	M. Schumacher	M. Hakkinen	D. Coulthard
'01	R. Schumacher	D. Coulthard	R. Barrichello
'02	M. Schumacher	R. Barrichello	R. Schumacher
'03	M. Schumacher	K. Raikkonen	R. Barrichello
'04	M. Schumacher	J. Button	J.P. Montoya

Results

	DRIVER	CAR	KPH	GAP
1	F. Alonso	Renault	209,085	-
2	M. Schumacher	Ferrari	209,077	0'00"215
3	J. Button	BAR	208,670	0'10"481
4	A. Wurz	McLaren	207,996	0'27"554
5	T. Sato	BAR	207,712	0'34"783
6	J. Villeneuve	Sauber	206,556	1'04"442
7	J. Trulli	Toyota	206,330	1'10"258
8	N. Heidfeld	Williams	206,291	1'11"282
9	M. Webber	Williams	205,827	1'23"297
10	V. Liuzzi	Red Bull	205,809	1'23"764
11	R. Schumacher	Toyota	206,308	1'35"841
12	F. Massa	Sauber	205,646	1 lap
13	D. Coulthard	Red Bull	204,706	1 lap
14	N. Karthikeyan	Jordan	204,047	1 lap
15	T. Monteiro	Jordan	199,293	2 laps

RETIREMENTS

C. Albers	Minardi	20	Gearbox
R. Barrichello	Ferrari	18	Electrical
K. Raikkonen	McLaren	9	Axle-shaft
P. Friesacher	Minardi	8	Clutch
G. Fisichella	Renault	5	Spin

The Race

DRIVER	CAR	LAP	FASTEST LAP	TOP SPEED
M. Schumacher	Ferrari	48	1'21"858	315,4
J. Button	BAR	22	1'22"604	310,1
A. Wurz	McLaren	24	1'23"023	307,4
F. Alonso	Renault	22	1'23"133	311,5
K. Raikkonen	McLaren	8	1'23"296	299,5
T. Sato	BAR	23	1'23"368	310,0
V. Liuzzi	Red Bull	46	1'23"488	309,5
F. Massa	Sauber	37	1'23"602	314,5
N. Heidfeld	Williams	54	1'23"917	307,2
J. Villeneuve	Sauber	45	1'24"017	310,2
J. Trulli	Toyota	44	1'24"022	298,5
N. Karthikeyan	Jordan	20	1'24"094	307,9
R. Schumacher	Toyota	19	1'24"230	303,3
M. Webber	Williams	17	1'24"419	308,7
R. Barrichello	Ferrari	13	1'24"435	311,5
D. Coulthard	Red Bull	22	1'24"641	307,9
T. Monteiro	Jordan	19	1'24"719	302,6
G. Fisichella	Renault	4	1'25"665	308,2
C. Albers	Minardi	18	1'27"420	304,6
P. Friesacher	Minardi	5	1'28"334	306,8

SAN MARINO GP

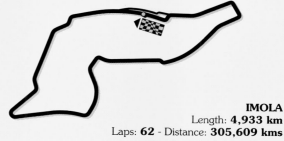

IMOLA
Length: **4,933 km**
Laps: **62** - Distance: **305,609 kms**

ALONSO HOLDS ON FOR THE WIN

Kimi Raikkonen took his first pole position at Imola to revitalize McLaren after their disappointing start to the season, which had been characterized by engine failures and a dose of bad luck.

Alongside was Alonso, followed by Button and Webber. The two Ferraris drivers were ninth on the grid with Barrichello and thirteenth with Schumacher, who had made an incredible mistake at the Rivazza in the second qualifying session. With Montoya still absent, McLaren gave their number two drive to Alexander Wurz, whose last race was the 2000 Malaysian GP with Benetton.

Raikkonen got a good start to power into the lead of the race ahead of Alonso, but the gorgeous new McLaren was still having teething problems and this time a driveshaft failed on lap 9 forcing the Finn into retirement.

While Alonso was running a faultless race up front, no one appeared to notice that Schumacher was powering back into contention with a brilliant pit stop strategy and soon he was right behind the young Spanish charger.

Ross Brawn first delayed his pit stop and then Schummy showed his champion class with a series of quick laps so that when he returned to the track, he was right behind Alonso in second place, despite having only made one overtaking move throughout the entire race, on Button.

Once he had caught Alonso, the battle between the two drivers raged over the final 12 laps, sending the Ferrari fans wild. But Alonso was proving to be not only world class but also that he was not overawed by the German ace, and the Renault driver pulled out all the stops to hold off Schumacher despite being under considerable pressure in the closing stages.

Alonso and Schumacher took the flag in that order with just a few metres between them, a result that marked a symbolic handing over of the baton between the seven-times world champion and his young pretender for the title.

Third place went to Jenson Button, followed by Wurz who scored an excellent fourth on his F1 return, and Sato in the other BAR. However the two BARs were thought to be under the minimum weight limit when weighed without fuel and the San Marino GP came to a close with the possibility of a change in the final results.

The discovery that BAR were apparently using an extra fuel tank to act as ballast cost them the cancellation of their 10 points gained at Imola and a disqualification for the next two races.
The FIA ruling was accepted by BAR, which preferred not to lodge an appeal to avoid creating any further damage to the image of the Anglo-Japanese team.

Despite a superb late recovery by Schumacher, cheered on by the Ferrari tifosi, Alonso held on to the lead of the race and took the chequered flag in the San Marino GP. Note the anxiety, worry and then the joy on Flavio Briatore's face.

	CHAMPIONSHIPS POINTS	AUSTRALIAN GP	MALAYSIAN GP	BAHRAIN GP	SAN MARINO GP	SPANISH GP	MONACO GP	EUROPEAN GP	CANADIAN GP	UNITED STATES GP	FRENCH GP	BRITISH GP	GERMAN GP	HUNGARIAN GP	TURKISH GP	ITALIAN GP	BELGIUM GP	BRAZILIAN GP	JAPANESE GP	CHINA GP	TOTAL POINT
1	F. ALONSO	6	10	10	10																36
2	J. TRULLI	-	8	8	4																20
3	G. FISICHELLA	10	-	-	-																10
4	M. SCHUMACHER	-	2	-	8																10
5	R. SCHUMACHER	-	4	5	-																9
6	D. COULTHARD	5	3	1	-																9
7	M. WEBBER	4	-	3	2																9
8	N. HEIDFELD	-	6	-	3																9
9	J. VILLENEUVE	-	-	-	5																5
10	R. BARRICHELLO	8	-	-																	8
11	J.P. MONTOYA	3	5	/	/																8
12	K. RAIKKONEN	1	-	6	-																7
13	A. WURZ	/	/	/	6																6
14	P. DE LA ROSA	/	/	4	/																4
15	C. KLIEN	2	1	-	/																3
16	F. MASSA	-	-	2	-																2
17	V. LIUZZI	/	/	/	1																1
18	T. SATO	-	-	-	sq.																0
19	J. BUTTON	-	-	-	sq.																0
20	T. MONTEIRO	-	-	-	-																0
21	N. KARTHIKEYAN	-	-	-	-																0
22	P. FRIESACHER	-	-	-	-																0
23	C. ALBERS	-	-	-	-																0
24	A. DAVIDSON	/	-	/	/																0

sq.: Disqualified

POLE POSITION

'90	A. Senna	'98	M. Hakkinen
'91	G. Berger	'99	M. Hakkinen
'92	N. Mansell	'00	M. Schumacher
'93	A. Prost	'01	M. Schumacher
'94	M. Schumacher	'02	M. Schumacher
'95	M. Schumacher	'03	M. Schumacher
'96	D. Hill	'04	M. Schumacher
'97	J. Villeneuve	'05	K. Raikkonen

STARTING GRID

1
 KIMI RAIKKONEN McLaren
 MARK WEBBER Williams

2
 FERNANDO ALONSO Renault
 RALF SCHUMACHER Toyota

3
 JARNO TRULLI Toyota
 GIANCARLO FISICHELLA Renault

4
 JUAN PABLO MONTOYA McLaren
 MICHAEL SCHUMACHER Ferrari

5
 DAVID COULTHARD Red Bull
 FELIPE MASSA Sauber

6
 VITANTONIO LIUZZI Red Bull
 JACQUES VILLENEUVE Sauber

7
 NARAIN KARTHIKEYAN Jordan
 CHRISTIJAN ALBERS Minardi

8
 PATRICK FRIESACHER Minardi
 RUBENS BARRICHELLO Ferrari

9
 NICK HEIDFELD Williams
 TIAGO MONTEIRO Jordan

10

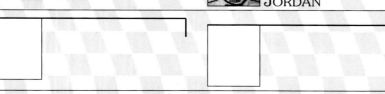

	1°	2°	3°
'90	A. Prost	N. Mansell	A. Nannini
'91	N. Mansell	A. Prost	R. Patrese
'92	N. Mansell	M. Schumacher	J. Alesi
'93	A. Prost	A. Senna	M. Schumacher
'94	D. Hill	M. Schumacher	M. Brundell
'95	M. Schumacher	J. Herbert	G. Berger
'96	M. Schumacher	J. Alesi	J. Villeneuve
'97	J. Villeneuve	O. Panis	J. Alesi
'98	M. Hakkinen	D. Coulthard	M. Schumacher
'99	M. Hakkinen	D. Coulthard	M. Schumacher
'00	M. Hakkinen	D. Coulthard	R. Barrichello
'01	M. Schumacher	J.P. Montoya	J. Villeneuve
'02	M. Schumacher	J.P. Montoya	D. Coulthard
'03	M. Schumacher	F. Alonso	R. Barrichello
'04	M. Schumacher	R. Barrichello	J. Trulli

RESULTS

	DRIVER	CAR	KPH	GAP
1	K. Raikkonen	McLaren	209,844	-
2	F. Alonso	Renault	208,742	0'27"652
3	J. Trulli	Toyota	208,019	0'45"947
4	R. Schumacher	Toyota	207,989	0'46"719
5	G. Fisichella	Renault	207,548	0'57"936
6	M. Webber	Williams	207,133	1'08"542
7	J.P. Montoya	McLaren	206,655	1 lap
8	D. Coulthard	Red Bull	206,569	1 lap
9	R. Barrichello	Ferrari	206,511	1 lap
10	N. Heidfeld	Williams	206,483	1 lap
11	T. Monteiro	Jordan	198,625	3 laps
12	N. Karthikeyan	Jordan	197,654	3 laps

RETIREMENTS

F. Massa	Sauber	63	Wheel
J. Villeneuve	Sauber	51	Hydraulic circuit
M. Schumacher	Ferrari	46	Wheel
C. Albers	Minardi	19	Gearbox
P. Friesacher	Minardi	11	Spin
V. Liuzzi	Red Bull	9	Spin

THE RACE

DRIVER	CAR	LAP	FASTEST LAP	TOP SPEED
G. Fisichella	Renault	66	1'15"641	327,3
M. Schumacher	Ferrari	31	1'15"648	325,6
J.P. Montoya	McLaren	55	1'15"771	325,0
K. Raikkonen	McLaren	41	1'15"977	326,5
F. Alonso	Renault	59	1'16"098	326,7
R. Schumacher	Toyota	63	1'16"469	325,4
N. Heidfeld	Williams	60	1'16"519	327,2
J. Trulli	Toyota	63	1'16"614	322,2
M. Webber	Williams	62	1'16"761	323,0
F. Massa	Sauber	51	1'16"802	326,1
D. Coulthard	Red Bull	65	1'16"947	325,4
R. Barrichello	Ferrari	64	1'17"156	329,1
J. Villeneuve	Sauber	43	1'17"585	328,8
T. Monteiro	Jordan	22	1'18"998	319,3
V. Liuzzi	Red Bull	9	1'19"435	324,6
N. Karthikeyan	Jordan	16	1'19"734	313,1
C. Albers	Minardi	15	1'20"124	325,6
P. Friesacher	Minardi	10	1'20"865	325,3
J. Button	BAR	-	-	-
T. Sato	BAR	-	-	-

SPANISH GP

RAIKKONEN FINALLY WINS!

Kimi Raikkonen grabbed his second pole position of the season in Spanish GP
qualifying, ahead of a splendid Webber and Alonso, who in turn was followed
by the two Toyotas. Schumacher was eighth and Barrichello had to start
from the back of the grid after a series of gearbox and engine problems.
At the start Raikkonen was quickest off the mark and immediately
took the lead, followed by Alonso and by Ralf Schumacher who got past
Webber in the Williams. While the Finn's domination continued up front,
second place was held by an unusually prudent Alonso who was maybe
worried about making a mistake in front of his home crowd,
and third and fourth were the two Toyotas of Schumacher and Trulli
who would overtake his German team-mate during the pit stop.
The race also saw the return of Montoya, who had recovered from his injured
shoulder, and who qualified and finished seventh, albeit one lap behind the
winner after having to make a double pit stop due to a faulty refuelling rig.
But it was Fisichella who had much more to recriminate than the Colombian.
The Italian ran a good race and would certainly have been on the podium,
maybe even ahead of Alonso, had he not been forced into the pits for
a lengthy stop to replace the front wing. Fisichella eventually finished fifth
ahead of Webber, Montoya and Coulthard in that order.
Alonso may have missed out on a home win in front of his fans
but second place was his fifth positive result in five races and it meant that he
was rapidly becoming the only real candidate for the 2005 Drivers' crown.

CATALUNYA
Length: **4,627 km**
Laps: **66** - Distance: **305,256 kms**

The talking-point this time is Ferrari's tyre problems,
which have marked the first part of the championship
for the Italian team and which became glaringly
obvious in Spain.
Barrichello took the chequered flag in ninth place
with his tyres totally worn out. Schumacher first punctured
his left rear on lap 44, stopped to change it and then
two laps later retired with an identical problem
with the front left tyre.

McLaren scored their first win of the year
with Kimi Raikkonen, at the home circuit
of Fernando Alonso, the leader of the world
championship after the first 4 races.

CHAMPIONSHIPS POINTS		AUSTRALIAN GP	MALAYSIAN GP	BAHRAIN GP	SAN MARINO GP	SPANISH GP	MONACO GP	EUROPEAN GP	CANADIAN GP	UNITED STATES GP	FRENCH GP	BRITISH GP	GERMAN GP	HUNGARIAN GP	TURKISH GP	ITALIAN GP	BELGIUM GP	BRAZILIAN GP	JAPANESE GP	CHINA GP	TOTAL POINT
1	F. ALONSO	6	10	10	10	8															44
2	J. TRULLI	-	8	8	4	6															26
3	K. RAIKKONEN	1	-	6	-	10															17
4	G. FISICHELLA	10	-	-	-	4															14
5	R. SCHUMACHER	-	4	5	-	5															14
6	M. WEBBER	4	-	3	2	3															12
7	M. SCHUMACHER	-	2	-	8	-															10
8	J.P. MONTOYA	3	5	/	/	2															10
9	D. COULTHARD	5	3	1	-	1															10
10	N. HEIDFELD	-	6	-	3	-															9
11	R. BARRICHELLO	8	-	-	-	-															8
12	A. WURZ	/	/	/	6	/															6
13	J. VILLENEUVE	-	-	-	5	-															5
14	P. DE LA ROSA	/	-	4	/	/															4
15	C. KLIEN	2	1	-	/	/															3
16	F. MASSA	-	-	2	-	-															2
17	V. LIUZZI	/	/	/	1	-															1
18	J. BUTTON	-	-	-	sq.	sq.															0
19	T. SATO	-	-	-	sq.	sq.															0
20	T. MONTEIRO	-	-	-	-	-															0
21	N. KARTHIKEYAN	-	-	-	-	-															0
22	P. FRIESACHER	-	-	-	-	-															0
23	C. ALBERS	-	-	-	-	-															0
24	A. DAVIDSON	/	-	/	/	/															0

sq.: Disqualified

POLE POSITION

STARTING GRID

	1°	2°	3°
'90	A. Senna	J. Alesi	G. Berger
'91	A. Senna	N. Mansell	J. Alesi
'92	A. Senna	N. Mansell	R. Patrese
'93	A. Senna	D. Hill	J. Alesi
'94	M. Schumacher	M. Brundle	G. Berger
'95	M. Schumacher	D. Hill	G. Berger
'96	O. Panis	D. Coulthard	J. Herbert
'97	M. Schumacher	R. Barrichello	E. Irvine
'98	M. Hakkinen	G. Fisichella	E. Irvine
'99	M. Schumacher	E. Irvine	M. Hakkinen
'00	D. Coulthard	R. Barrichello	G. Fisichella
'01	M. Schumacher	R. Barrichello	E. Irvine
'02	D. Coulthard	M. Schumacher	R. Schumacher
'03	J.P. Montoya	K. Raikkonen	M. Schumacher
'04	J. Trulli	J. Button	R. Barrichello

1

 KIMI RAIKKONEN McLAREN

 FERNANDO ALONSO RENAULT

2

 MARK WEBBER WILLIAMS

 GIANCARLO FISICHELLA RENAULT

3

 JARNO TRULLI TOYOTA

 NICK HEIDFELD WILLIAMS

4

 DAVID COULTHARD RED BULL

 MICHAEL SCHUMACHER FERRARI

5

 JACQUES VILLENEUVE SAUBER

 RUBENS BARRICHELLO FERRARI

6

 FELIPE MASSA SAUBER

 VITANTONIO LIUZZI RED BULL

7

 PATRICK FRIESACHER MINARDI

 CHRISTIJAN ALBERS MINARDI

8

 TIAGO MONTEIRO JORDAN

 JUAN PABLO MONTOYA McLAREN

9

 NARAIN KARTHIKEYAN JORDAN

 RALF SCHUMACHER TOYOTA

10

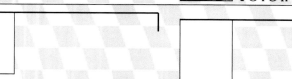

RESULTS

	DRIVER	CAR	KPH	GAP
1	K. Raikkonen	McLaren	148,501	-
2	N. Heidfeld	Williams	148,176	0'13"877
3	M. Webber	Williams	148,068	0'18"484
4	F. Alonso	Renault	147,648	0'36"487
5	J.P. Montoya	McLaren	147,645	0'36"647
6	R. Schumacher	Toyota	147,632	0'37"177
7	M. Schumacher	Ferrari	147,631	0'37"223
8	R. Barrichello	Ferrari	147,623	0'37"570
9	F. Massa	Sauber	145,492	1 lap
10	J. Trulli	Toyota	145,249	1 lap
11	J. Villeneuve	Sauber	145,238	1 lap
12	G. Fisichella	Renault	144,627	1 lap
13	T. Monteiro	Jordan	141,104	3 lap
14	C. Albers	Minardi	137,577	5 laps

RETIREMENTS

V. Liuzzi	Red Bull	59	Wheel
P. Friesacher	Minardi	29	Spin
D. Coulthard	Red Bull	23	Accident
N. Karthikeyan	Jordan	28	Accident

THE RACE

DRIVER	CAR	LAP	FASTEST LAP	TOP SPEED
M. Schumacher	Ferrari	40	1'15"842	300,2
K. Raikkonen	McLaren	41	1'15"921	298,0
F. Alonso	Renault	19	1'16"600	299,6
G. Fisichella	Renault	20	1'16"776	299,3
J. Trulli	Toyota	38	1'16"812	289,7
R. Barrichello	Ferrari	51	1'16"916	298,4
M. Webber	Williams	77	1'16"971	296,8
R. Schumacher	Toyota	11	1'17"070	292,9
N. Heidfeld	Williams	15	1'17"159	296,7
J.P. Montoya	McLaren	50	1'17"403	298,9
J. Villeneuve	Sauber	17	1'17"482	295,0
D. Coulthard	Red Bull	15	1'17"693	291,6
F. Massa	Sauber	16	1'17"799	301,1
V. Liuzzi	Red Bull	43	1'18"030	290,7
P. Friesacher	Minardi	19	1'19"037	294,5
C. Albers	Minardi	22	1'20"237	291,4
T. Monteiro	Jordan	12	1'20"747	284,2
N. Karthikeyan	Jordan	14	1'22"019	285,0
J. Button	BAR	-	-	-
T. Sato	BAR	-	-	-

MONACO GP

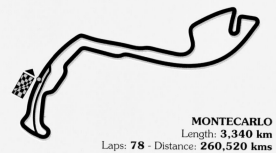

MONTECARLO
Length: **3,340 km**
Laps: **78** - Distance: **260,520 kms**

WILLIAMS RENAISSANCE

It was Raikkonen who again dominated qualifying for McLaren at the Monte Carlo street circuit; Alonso was second, albeit just a fraction behind the Finn. Fisichella and Trulli were next up, while the two Ferraris as usual were half-way down the grid.

Two nasty crashes in qualifying relegated Ralf Schumacher to the back of the grid together with Montoya, who was penalized for reckless driving for his part in a pile-up involving Ralf Schumacher, Coulthard and Villeneuve. Kimi got the best start to move into the lead and he would hold that lead right until the chequered flag. The Finn drove a clean, precise and faultless race and fully deserved his win. Behind him, Alonso and Fisichella looked as if they might be able to do something about the McLaren domination in the early stages, but their attack soon fizzled out.

It was a disappointing Monaco GP for the two Renaults, which were afflicted by serious tyre trouble as well as errors committed by the team. On lap 25 both cars came into the pits at the same time and the Italian had to wait until Alonso had finished refuelling, losing 25 seconds. The confusion was created by the entry of the safety car following Albers' crash at Mirabeau where his Minardi ended up by blocking the track.

In the chain reaction that followed Schumacher lost his front wing and ran into the back of the Red Bull of Coulthard, who had to retire with rear wing and suspension damage.

While all this was going on, the McLaren team managed to keep a cool head and they kept Raikkonen out on the track behind the safety car. On the restart the Finn, with a clear road and a lightened fuel load, immediately put in a string of quick laps. He only made one pit stop on his way to a well-deserved win and was followed home by the two Williams of Heidfeld and Webber, who scored his first-ever podium finish.

Fourth was Alonso who despite everything managed to hold off late attacks from Montoya and Ralf Schumacher.

Mercedes notched up its 200th GP as engine supplier at Monte Carlo. They started supplying engines in 1994 with Sauber and then continued with McLaren, with whom they won their first GP in Australia in 1997 with David Coulthard behind the wheel.
They subsequently won the Drivers' title with Hakkinen in 1998 and 1999 and the Constructors' title in 1998.

A fascinating circuit, so different from all the others in the world championship. Barriers and guard-rails surround the entire circuit, leaving no run-off areas, luxurious yachts, gorgeous women sunbathing on balconies, terraces and boats ... all this is Monaco.

CHAMPIONSHIPS POINTS	AUSTRALIAN GP	MALAYSIAN GP	BAHRAIN GP	SAN MARINO GP	SPANISH GP	MONACO GP	EUROPEAN GP	CANADIAN GP	UNITED STATES GP	FRENCH GP	BRITISH GP	GERMAN GP	HUNGARIAN GP	TURKISH GP	ITALIAN GP	BELGIUM GP	BRAZILIAN GP	JAPANESE GP	CHINA GP	TOTAL POINT
1 F. ALONSO	6	10	10	10	8	5														49
2 K. RAIKKONEN	1	-	6	-	10	10														27
3 J. TRULLI	-	8	8	4	6	-														26
4 M. WEBBER	4	-	3	2	3	6														18
5 N. HEIDFELD	-	6	-	3	-	8														17
6 R. SCHUMACHER	-	4	5	-	5	3														17
7 G. FISICHELLA	10	-	-	-	4	-														14
8 J.P. MONTOYA	3	5	/	/	2	4														14
9 M. SCHUMACHER	-	2	-	8	-	2														12
10 D. COULTHARD	5	3	1	-	1	-														10
11 R. BARRICHELLO	8	-	-	-	-	1														9
12 A. WURZ	/	/	/	6	/	/														6
13 J. VILLENEUVE	-	-	-	5	-	-														5
14 P. DE LA ROSA	/	/	4	/	/	/														4
15 C. KLIEN	2	1	-	/	/	/														3
16 F. MASSA	-	-	2	-	-	-														2
17 V. LIUZZI	/	/	/	1	-	-														1
18 J. BUTTON	-	-	-	sq.	sq.	sq.														0
19 T. SATO	-	-	-	sq.	sq.	sq.														0
20 T. MONTEIRO	-	-	-	-	-	-														0
21 N. KARTHIKEYAN	-	-	-	-	-	-														0
22 P. FRIESACHER	-	-	-	-	-	-														0
23 C. ALBERS	-	-	-	-	-	-														0
24 A. DAVIDSON	/	-	/	/	/	/														0

sq.: Disqualified

POLE POSITION

'90	-	'98	-
'91	-	'99	H.H. Frentzen
'92	-	'00	D. Coulthard
'93	A. Prost	'01	M. Schumacher
'94	M. Schumacher	'02	J.P. Montoya
'95	D. Coulthard	'03	K. Raikkonen
'96	D. Hill	'04	M. Schumacher
'97	J. Villeneuve	'05	N. Heidfeld

STARTING GRID

1
 NICK HEIDFELD — WILLIAMS
 KIMI RAIKKONEN — MCLAREN

2
 MARK WEBBER — WILLIAMS
 JARNO TRULLI — TOYOTA

3
 JUAN PABLO MONTOYA — MCLAREN
 FERNANDO ALONSO — RENAULT

4
 RUBENS BARRICHELLO — FERRARI
 RALF SCHUMACHER — TOYOTA

5
 GIANCARLO FISICHELLA — RENAULT
 MICHAEL SCHUMACHER — FERRARI

6
 FELIPE MASSA — SAUBER
 DAVID COULTHARD — RED BULL

7
 JENSON BUTTON — BAR
 VITANTONIO LIUZZI — RED BULL

8
 JACQUES VILLENEUVE — SAUBER
 TAKUMA SATO — BAR

9
 TIAGO MONTEIRO — JORDAN
 PATRICK FRIESACHER — MINARDI

10
 NARAIN KARTHIKEYAN — JORDAN
 CHRISTIJAN ALBERS — MINARDI

	1°	2°	3°
'90	-	-	-
'91	-	-	-
'92	-	-	-
'93	A. Senna	D. Hill	A. Prost
'94	M. Schumacher	D. Hill	M. Hakkinen
'95	M. Schumacher	J. Alesi	D. Coulthard
'96	J. Villeneuve	M. Schumacher	D. Coulthard
'97	M. Hakkinen	D. Coulthard	J. Villeneuve
'98	-	-	-
'99	J. Herbert	J. Trulli	R. Barrichello
'00	M. Schumacher	M. Hakkinen	D. Coulthard
'01	M. Schumacher	J.P. Montoya	D. Coulthard
'02	R. Barrichello	M. Schumacher	K. Raikkonen
'03	R. Schumacher	J.P. Montoya	R. Barrichello
'04	M. Schumacher	R. Barrichello	J. Button

RESULTS

	DRIVER	CAR	KPH	GAP
1	F. Alonso	Renault	198,555	-
2	N. Heidfeld	Williams	197,959	0'16"567
3	R. Barrichello	Ferrari	197,888	0'18"549
4	D. Coulthard	Red Bull	197,422	0'31"588
5	M. Schumacher	Ferrari	196,752	0'50"445
6	G. Fisichella	Renault	196,700	0'51"932
7	J.P. Montoya	McLaren	196,479	0'58"173
8	J. Trulli	Toyota	196,024	1'11"091
9	V. Liuzzi	Red Bull	196,009	1'11"529
10	J. Button	BAR	195,160	1'35"786
11	T. Sato	BAR	195,131	1 lap
12	J. Villeneuve	Sauber	194,168	1 lap
13	F. Massa	Sauber	193,568	1 lap
14	T. Monteiro	Jordan	192,232	1 lap
15	N. Karthikeyan	Jordan	192,200	1 lap
16	C. Albers	Minardi	188,650	2 laps
17	P. Friesacher	Minardi	187,487	3 laps

RETIREMENTS

K. Raikkonen	McLaren	58	Suspension
R. Schumacher	Toyota	33	Spin
M. Webber	Williams	0	Accident

THE RACE

DRIVER	CAR	LAP	FASTEST LAP	TOP SPEED
F. Alonso	Renault	44	1'30"711	311,5
K. Raikkonen	McLaren	9	1'30"940	306,9
R. Barrichello	Ferrari	44	1'31"028	313,1
N. Heidfeld	Williams	9	1'31"124	306,8
D. Coulthard	Red Bull	19	1'31"306	305,1
M. Schumacher	Ferrari	19	1'31"503	311,7
G. Fisichella	Renault	47	1'31"708	311,6
R. Schumacher	Toyota	25	1'31"724	304,9
J. Trulli	Toyota	43	1'31"779	309,0
J.P. Montoya	McLaren	42	1'31"807	312,8
T. Sato	BAR	26	1'31"889	309,2
J. Button	BAR	20	1'31"955	308,3
V. Liuzzi	Red Bull	43	1'31"971	308,8
F. Massa	Sauber	18	1'32"329	309,1
J. Villeneuve	Sauber	41	1'32"583	308,3
N. Karthikeyan	Jordan	21	1'33"292	305,2
T. Monteiro	Jordan	39	1'33"425	303,9
C. Albers	Minardi	18	1'35"047	307,2
P. Friesacher	Minardi	18	1'35"536	301,0
M. Webber	Williams	-	-	-

EUROPEAN GP

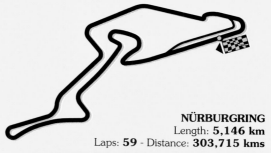

NÜRBURGRING
Length: **5,146 km**
Laps: **59** - Distance: **303,715 kms**

NO LUCK FOR KIMI

For the first time in his career and after 90 GPs,
Nick Heidfeld set pole position on his home circuit of the Nürburgring,
a result that helped galvanize the struggling Williams team.
Heidfeld was followed by Raikkonen, who was on a roll after two successive wins,
Webber with the second Williams and Trulli. Championship leader Alonso was
only sixth, and the Spaniard had opted to start with a heavy fuel load.
The German got off to a bad start however and was passed by Raikkonen, while
behind the Finn Webber caused chaos by colliding with Montoya in an incident
that also involved the two Schumacher brothers, Barrichello and Villeneuve.
Raikkonen was leading the race with incredible determination, possibly too much,
despite having a good lead over second and third-placed Heidfeld and Coulthard.
He was attacking the kerbs, delaying his braking until as late as possible,
and it was this that eventually caused his downfall.
The vibrations caused by going over the kerbs had an effect on his McLaren's
stability and the suspension. Alonso was gaining rapidly and Raikkonen
was losing seconds to the Spaniard every lap. There were frenetic
communications between the driver and the engineers on the pit wall because
no one was sure whether keeping the driver out on the track was a risk or not.
Raikkonen went for it, but on the final lap his suspension collapsed and his
McLaren went slamming into the guard-rail, luckily without injury for the driver.
Alonso found victory handed to him on a silver plate, and he was followed
by Heidfeld, who made the podium for the second time this year,
and by Barrichello in third.
Fourth was Coulthard, who missed out on the podium after being penalised with
a 'drive-through' for exceeding the speed limit in the pit lane during his stop.

HIGHLIGHTS

After setting fourth quickest time in qualifying,
it was a disappointing weekend for Jarno Trulli. Before
the race got underway his Toyota had ignition problems
and his mechanics had to take to the grid to get it to start.
The race stewards were unwavering and slapped the
penalty on him, so from third place Jarno slipped down
to ninth. He picked up a point in the standings by beating
Vitantonio Liuzzi with the Red Bull to the line.

PHOTO PORTFOLIO

Being back home helped German Nick Heidfeld
to the pole position and second place at the finish.
Victory once again went to Alonso, even though
the moral winner was Raikkonen, who led the race
until the final lap when his McLaren's suspension
collapsed and he had to retire.

CHAMPIONSHIPS POINTS		AUSTRALIAN GP	MALAYSIAN GP	BAHRAIN GP	SAN MARINO GP	SPANISH GP	MONACO GP	EUROPEAN GP	CANADIAN GP	UNITED STATES GP	FRENCH GP	BRITISH GP	GERMAN GP	HUNGARIAN GP	TURKISH GP	ITALIAN GP	BELGIUM GP	BRAZILIAN GP	JAPANESE GP	CHINA GP	TOTAL POINT
1	F. ALONSO	6	10	10	10	8	5	10														59
2	K. RAIKKONEN	1	-	6	-	10	10	-														27
3	J. TRULLI	-	8	8	4	6	-	1														27
4	N. HEIDFELD	-	6	-	3	-	8	8														25
5	M. WEBBER	4	-	3	2	3	6	-														18
6	R. SCHUMACHER	-	4	5	-	5	3	-														17
7	G. FISICHELLA	10	-	-	-	4	-	3														17
8	M. SCHUMACHER	-	2	-	8	-	2	4														16
9	J.P. MONTOYA	3	5	/	/	2	4	2														16
10	D. COULTHARD	5	3	1	-	1	-	5														15
11	R. BARRICHELLO	8	-	-	-	-	1	6														15
12	A. WURZ	/	/	/	6	/	/	/														6
13	J. VILLENEUVE	-	-	-	5	-	-	-														5
14	P. DE LA ROSA	/	/	4	/	/	/	/														4
15	C. KLIEN	2	1	-	/	/	/	/														3
16	F. MASSA	-	-	2	-	-	-	-														2
17	V. LIUZZI	/	/	/	1	-	-	-														1
18	J. BUTTON	-	-	-	sq.	sq.	sq.	-														0
19	T. SATO	-	-	-	sq.	sq.	sq.	-														0
20	T. MONTEIRO	-	-	-	-	-	-	-														0
21	N. KARTHIKEYAN	-	-	-	-	-	-	-														0
22	P. FRIESACHER	-	-	-	-	-	-	-														0
23	C. ALBERS	-	-	-	-	-	-	-														0
24	A. DAVIDSON	/	-	/	/	/	/	/														0

sq.: Disqualified

POLE POSITION

'90	A. Senna	'98	D. Coulthard
'91	R. Patrese	'99	M. Schumacher
'92	A. Senna	'00	M. Schumacher
'93	A. Prost	'01	M. Schumacher
'94	M. Schumacher	'02	J.P. Montoya
'95	M. Schumacher	'03	R. Schumacher
'96	D. Hill	'04	R. Schumacher
'97	M. Schumacher	'05	J. Button

	1°	2°	3°
'90	A. Senna	N. Piquet	N. Mansell
'91	N. Piquet	S. Modena	R. Patrese
'92	G. Berger	M. Schumacher	J. Alesi
'93	A. Prost	M. Schumacher	D. Hill
'94	M. Schumacher	D. Hill	J. Alesi
'95	J. Alesi	R. Barrichello	E. Irvine
'96	D. Hill	J. Villeneuve	J. Alesi
'97	M. Schumacher	J. Alesi	G. Fisichella
'98	M. Schumacher	G. Fisichella	E. Irvine
'99	M. Hakkinen	G. Fisichella	E. Irvine
'00	M. Schumacher	R. Barrichello	G. Fisichella
'01	R. Schumacher	M. Schumacher	M. Hakkinen
'02	M. Schumacher	D. Coulthard	R. Barrichello
'03	M. Schumacher	R. Schumacher	J.P. Montoya
'04	M. Schumacher	R. Barrichello	J. Button

STARTING GRID

Pos		
1	JENSON BUTTON — BAR	MICHAEL SCHUMACHER — FERRARI
2	FERNANDO ALONSO — RENAULT	GIANCARLO FISICHELLA — RENAULT
3	JUAN PABLO MONTOYA — McLAREN	TAKUMA SATO — BAR
4	KIMI RAIKKONEN — McLAREN	JACQUES VILLENEUVE — SAUBER
5	JARNO TRULLI — TOYOTA	RALF SCHUMACHER — TOYOTA
6	FELIPE MASSA — SAUBER	DAVID COULTHARD — RED BULL
7	NICK HEIDFELD — WILLIAMS	MARK WEBBER — WILLIAMS
8	CHRISTIJAN ALBERS — MINARDI	CHRISTIAN KLIEN — RED BULL
9	NARAIN KARTHIKEYAN — JORDAN	TIAGO MONTEIRO — JORDAN
10	PATRICK FRIESACHER — MINARDI	RUBENS BARRICHELLO — FERRARI

RESULTS

	DRIVER	CAR	KPH	GAP
1	K. Raikkonen	McLaren	198,754	-
2	M. Schumacher	Ferrari	198,713	0'01"137
3	R. Barrichello	Ferrari	197,310	0'40"483
4	F. Massa	Sauber	196,792	0'55"139
5	M. Webber	Williams	196,769	0'55"779
6	R. Schumacher	Toyota	195,035	1 lap
7	D. Coulthard	Red Bull	194,681	1 lap
8	C. Klien	Red Bull	194,449	1 lap
9	J. Villeneuve	Sauber	194,435	1 lap
10	T. Monteiro	Jordan	189,987	3 laps
11	C. Albers	Minardi	189,639	3 laps

RETIREMENTS

J. Trulli	Toyota	62	Brakes
J.P. Montoya	McLaren	52	Black flag
J. Button	BAR	46	Crashed
N. Heidfeld	Williams	43	Engine
T. Sato	BAR	40	Brakes
P. Friesacher	Minardi	39	Hydraulic circuit
F. Alonso	Renault	38	Crashed
G. Fisichella	Renault	32	Hydraulic circuit
N. Karthikeyan	Jordan	24	Crashed

THE RACE

DRIVER	CAR	LAP	FASTEST LAP	TOP SPEED
K. Raikkonen	McLaren	23	1'14"384	333,0
J.P. Montoya	McLaren	24	1'14"576	331,4
F. Alonso	Renault	38	1'14"727	335,8
M. Schumacher	Ferrari	32	1'14"868	338,4
G. Fisichella	Renault	24	1'14"890	338,3
J. Button	BAR	30	1'15"189	325,1
M. Webber	Williams	23	1'15"401	336,6
R. Barrichello	Ferrari	46	1'15"480	336,7
N. Heidfeld	Williams	20	1'15"752	333,6
R. Schumacher	Toyota	44	1'15"827	335,1
J. Trulli	Toyota	43	1'15"872	332,2
J. Villeneuve	Sauber	26	1'15"945	332,2
F. Massa	Sauber	18	1'16"008	330,9
T. Sato	BAR	14	1'16"044	323,4
C. Klien	Red Bull	46	1'16"299	331,3
D. Coulthard	Red Bull	17	1'16"414	328,0
N. Karthikeyan	Jordan	20	1'17"015	325,1
T. Monteiro	Jordan	19	1'17"344	326,0
C. Albers	Minardi	15	1'18"462	330,0
P. Friesacher	Minardi	33	1'18"709	328,1

CANADIAN GP

RAIKKONEN'S REVENGE

Pole position in Canada went to Button for the second time in his career,
Schumacher was alongside and the two Renaults of Alonso
and Fisichella were right behind on the second row.
The final grid position was taken up by Barrichello,
who was getting used to starting from the back.
At the lights Fisichella rocketed away and took the lead followed by Alonso.
The Italian driver was on top form and led the race until half distance, when his
Renault stopped in the pits with a hydraulic problem. It was another unfortunate
race for the Italian, who won the opening round of the season in Australia.
Now it was Alonso who looked as if he was heading for an easy win,
but on lap 40 Fernando made a rare mistake and hit the wall.
Montoya took over at the front and the Colombian held the lead
for almost ten laps, followed by team-mate Raikkonen.
But just like Fisichella, it was not Montoya's day either and the Colombian's race
was ruined by the entry of the safety car onto the track following Button's crash.
Confusion reigned supreme, in particular in the McLaren garage, as the cars
unexpectedly returned to the pits. First the Anglo-German team called
in Raikkonen before Montoya and then the Colombian raged away from the
pits without realising that the red light at the end of the pit lane was still on.
To make matters worse Montoya then overtook Coulthard while the safety car
was out and the FIA stewards decided to black-flag him.
So Raikkonen wiped the slate clean after his dramatic DNF in the previous
race by taking the win and the maximum points, and the Finn was followed
by the two Ferraris of Schumacher and Barrichello, who finished on the podium
in second and third. In particular the Brazilian put in an incredible drive
up through the field from the back of the grid.

GILLES VILLENEUVE
Length: **4,361 km**
Laps: **70** - Distance: **305,270 kms**

Narain Karthikeyan, the first Indian in Formula 1,
might be a nice guy but he is rapidly turning into a bit
of a nightmare for his fellow F1 drivers.
In the previous GP at the Nürburgring he got on
Villeneuve's nerves with a bit of fairing-bashing, to the
point where the Canadian asked him if he thought he was
still driving go-karts; while in Canada he put on an amazing
display of off-road driving, corner-cutting and a series
of impossible braking manoeuvres.

Two Renaults took the front row of the grid in
qualifying at the delightful Montreal circuit, named
after Gilles Villeneuve and situated in the park
alongside the lake shore. But in the race they
were both forced to retire. Raikkonen won in
the McLaren, which was becoming more and more
competitive in every race.

CHAMPIONSHIPS POINTS	AUSTRALIAN GP	MALAYSIAN GP	BAHRAIN GP	SAN MARINO GP	SPANISH GP	MONACO GP	EUROPEAN GP	CANADIAN GP	UNITED STATES GP	FRENCH GP	BRITISH GP	GERMAN GP	HUNGARIAN GP	TURKISH GP	ITALIAN GP	BELGIUM GP	BRAZILIAN GP	JAPANESE GP	CHINA GP	TOTAL POINT
1 F. ALONSO	6	10	10	10	8	5	10	-												59
2 K. RAIKKONEN	1	-	6	-	10	10	-	10												37
3 J. TRULLI	-	8	8	4	6	-	1	-												27
4 N. HEIDFELD	-	6	-	3	-	8	8	-												25
5 M. SCHUMACHER	-	2	-	8	-	2	4	8												24
6 M. WEBBER	4	-	3	2	3	6	-	4												22
7 R. BARRICHELLO	8	-	-	-	-	1	6	6												21
8 R. SCHUMACHER	-	4	5	-	5	3	-	3												20
9 G. FISICHELLA	10	-	-	-	4	-	3	-												17
10 D. COULTHARD	5	3	1	-	1	-	5	2												17
11 J.P. MONTOYA	3	5	/	/	2	4	2	sq.												16
12 F. MASSA	-	-	2	-	-	-	-	5												7
13 A. WURZ	/	/	/	6	/	/	/	/												6
14 J. VILLENEUVE	-	-	-	5	-	-	-	-												5
15 P. DE LA ROSA	/	/	4	/	/	/	/	/												4
16 C. KLIEN	2	1	-	/	/	/	-	1												4
17 V. LIUZZI	/	/	/	1	-	-	-	-												1
18 J. BUTTON	-	-	-	sq.	sq.	sq.	-	-												0
19 T. SATO	-	-	-	sq.	sq.	sq.	-	-												0
20 T. MONTEIRO	-	-	-	-	-	-	-	-												0
21 N. KARTHIKEYAN	-	-	-	-	-	-	-	-												0
22 P. FRIESACHER	-	-	-	-	-	-	-	-												0
23 C. ALBERS	-	-	-	-	-	-	-	-												0
24 A. DAVIDSON	/	-	/	/	/	/	/	/												0

sq.: Disqualified

POLE POSITION

'90	-	'98	-
'91	-	'99	-
'92	-	'00	M. Schumacher
'93	-	'01	M. Schumacher
'94	-	'02	M. Schumacher
'95	-	'03	K. Raikkonen
'96	-	'04	R. Barrichello
'97	-	'05	J. Trulli

STARTING GRID

1
 JARNO TRULLI TOYOTA
 KIMI RAIKKONEN McLAREN

2
 JENSON BUTTON BAR
 GIANCARLO FISICHELLA RENAULT

3
 MICHAEL SCHUMACHER FERRARI
 FERNANDO ALONSO RENAULT

4
 RUBENS BARRICHELLO FERRARI
 TAKUMA SATO BAR

5
 MARK WEBBER WILLIAMS
 FELIPE MASSA SAUBER

6
 JUAN PABLO MONTOYA McLAREN
 JACQUES VILLENEUVE SAUBER

7
 RICCARDO ZONTA TOYOTA
 CHRISTIAN KLIEN RED BULL

8
 NICK HEIDFELD WILLIAMS
 DAVID COULTHARD RED BULL

9
 TIAGO MONTEIRO JORDAN
 CHRISTIJAN ALBERS MINARDI

10
 NARAIN KARTHIKEYAN JORDAN
 PATRICK FRIESACHER MINARDI

	1°	2°	3°
'00	M. Schumacher	R. Barrichello	H.H. Frentzen
'01	M. Hakkinen	M. Schumacher	D. Coulthard
'02	R. Barrichello	M. Schumacher	D. Coulthard
'03	M. Schumacher	K. Raikkonen	H.H. Frentzen
'04	M. Schumacher	R. Barrichello	T. Sato

RESULTS

	DRIVER	CAR	KPH	GAP
1	M. Schumacher	Ferrari	204,648	-
2	R. Barrichello	Ferrari	204,590	0'01"522
3	T. Monteiro	Jordan	201,558	1 lap
4	N. Karthikeyan	Jordan	200,401	1 lap
5	C. Albers	Minardi	197,386	2 laps
6	P. Friesacher	Minardi	196,821	2 laps

RETIREMENTS

J. Button	BAR	0	Did not start
M. Webber	Williams	0	Did not start
J. Villeneuve	Sauber	0	Did not start
J. Trulli	Toyota	0	Did not start
G. Fisichella	Renault	0	Did not start
J.P. Montoya	McLaren	0	Did not start
C. Klien	Red Bull	0	Did not start
F. Alonso	Renault	0	Did not start
K. Raikkonen	McLaren	0	Did not start
D. Coulthard	Red Bull	0	Did not start
T. Sato	BAR	0	Did not start
N. Heidfeld	Williams	0	Did not start
F. Massa	Sauber	0	Did not start
R. Zonta	Toyota	0	Did not start

THE RACE

DRIVER	CAR	LAP	FASTEST LAP	TOP SPEED
M. Schumacher	Ferrari	48	1'11"497	339,5
R. Barrichello	Ferrari	48	1'11"649	343,0
T. Monteiro	Jordan	44	1'13"237	333,6
N. Karthikeyan	Jordan	65	1'13"370	336,3
C. Albers	Minardi	2	1'13"907	336,8
P. Friesacher	Minardi	43	1'14"490	337,9
J. Button	BAR	-	-	-
M. Webber	Williams	-	-	-
J. Villeneuve	Sauber	-	-	-
J. Trulli	Toyota	-	-	-
G. Fisichella	Renault	-	-	-
J.P. Montoya	McLaren	-	-	-
C. Klien	Red Bull	-	-	-
F. Alonso	Renault	-	-	-
K. Raikkonen	McLaren	-	-	-
D. Coulthard	Red Bull	-	-	-
T. Sato	BAR	-	-	-
N. Heidfeld	Williams	-	-	-
F. Massa	Sauber	-	-	-
R. Zonta	Toyota	-	-	-

INDIANAPOLIS
Length: 4,192 km
Laps: 73 - Distance: 306,016 kms

INDIANAPOLIS FARCE

The cars lined up for their alignment lap. Off they went, zig-zagging to heat up the tyres. Another Formula 1 GP was about to start … but at the end of the lap, fourteen of the cars on the grid veered off into the pits and just six lined up for the lights. It was a pitiful spectacle, just six cars lost amidst the massive legendary Indianapolis oval. And yet it was real …

On went the lights, off they went, the two red Ferraris blasted away as if it was a real GP, followed by two Toyotas and two black Minardis. Not much can be said about the United States GP. Schumacher took the lead, followed like a shadow by Barrichello, Monteiro, Albers in the Minardi, Karthikeyan and Friesacher. The Indian driver took advantage of Albers' pit stop to nip into fourth place, which he held until the flag.

Lap after lap, the boos and jeers increased and so did the number of objects thrown onto the track by spectators, who were furious at the farce that was taking place before their very eyes. The drivers meanwhile were just trying not to ruin their engines in view of the next GP …

The only exciting moment, so to speak, was the duel between the two Ferraris on lap 52 when Schummy came out of the pit lane to find his team-mate alongside. Both drivers locked up the brakes and Barrichello was forced to go wide onto the grass.

The prize-giving ceremony, which was drowned out by booing and whistling, saw an incredulous Tiago Monteiro lift up the trophy for third place but there weren't the usual champagne celebrations.

It all came about following the decision by Michelin to advise its teams not to race because the tyres brought to Indianapolis were reckoned not to be safe on this type of track and the risk of incidents was thought to be too high. During Friday practice in fact, first Zonta (Toyota) had to stop after a tyre failure. Then Ralf Schumacher slammed into the wall, more or less at the same place as his crash the previous year; this time however he was lucky to emerge unhurt from the wreckage of his Toyota.

After that tyre trouble again afflicted Zonta, as well as Trulli, and even the Renaults and the McLarens had problems, despite not being involved in any crashes. At this point Michelin opted not to race.

It was a serious blow to the credibility of Formula 1, which for many years now has found it tough to endear itself to the American public.

Were faulty tyres to blame for Ralf Schumacher's crash and the problems of the other drivers? Or was it that tyre pressure was reduced to lower the cars for the ultra-quick banked curve before the main straight? Michelin boss Pierre Dupasquier would only say that "we do not know for sure and in any case in these conditions we cannot guarantee the safety of the drivers".

Call this a Grand Prix? Boos and jeers from the fans, frantic meetings between team managers and Bernie Ecclestone, futile attempts to find a stop-gap solution to get the GP to go ahead, and disappointment on the faces of everyone. The only one to celebrate was Tiago Monteiro, who finished third out of six starters to take the final podium place.

	CHAMPIONSHIPS POINTS	AUSTRALIAN GP	MALAYSIAN GP	BAHRAIN GP	SAN MARINO GP	SPANISH GP	MONACO GP	EUROPEAN GP	CANADIAN GP	UNITED STATES GP	FRENCH GP	BRITISH GP	GERMAN GP	HUNGARIAN GP	TURKISH GP	ITALIAN GP	BELGIUM GP	BRAZILIAN GP	JAPANESE GP	CHINA GP	TOTAL POINT
1	F. ALONSO	6	10	10	10	8	5	10	-	rit.											59
2	K. RAIKKONEN	1	-	6	-	10	10	-	10	rit.											37
3	M. SCHUMACHER	-	2	-	8	-	2	4	8	10											34
4	R. BARRICHELLO	8	-	-	-	1	6	6	8												29
5	J. TRULLI	-	8	8	4	6	-	1	-	rit.											27
6	N. HEIDFELD	-	6	-	3	-	8	8	-	rit.											25
7	M. WEBBER	4	-	3	2	3	6	-	4	rit.											22
8	R. SCHUMACHER	-	4	5	-	5	3	-	3	rit.											20
9	G. FISICHELLA	10	-	-	-	4	-	3	-	rit.											17
10	D. COULTHARD	5	3	1	-	1	-	5	2	rit.											17
11	J.P. MONTOYA	3	5	/	/	2	4	2	sq.	rit.											16
12	F. MASSA	-	-	2	-	-	-	-	5	rit.											7
13	T. MONTEIRO	-	-	-	-	-	-	-	-	6											6
14	A. WURZ	/	/	/	6	/	/	/	/	/											6
15	J. VILLENEUVE	-	-	-	5	-	-	-	-	rit.											5
16	N. KARTHIKEYAN	-	-	-	-	-	-	-	-	5											5
17	C. ALBERS	-	-	-	-	-	-	-	-	4											4
18	P. DE LA ROSA	/	-	4	/	/	/	/	/												4
19	C. KLIEN	2	1	-	/	/	/	/	1	rit.											4
20	P. FRIESACHER	-	-	-	-	-	-	-	-	3											3
21	V. LIUZZI	/	/	/	1	-	-	-	/	/											1
22	J. BUTTON	-	-	-	sq.	sq.	sq.	-	-	rit.											0
23	T. SATO	-	-	-	sq.	sq.	sq.	-	-	rit.											0
24	A. DAVIDSON	/	-	/	/	/	/	/	/												0

rit.: Retired   **sq.**: Disqualified

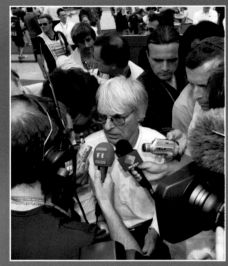

POLE POSITION

'90	N. Mansell	'98	M. Hakkinen
'91	R. Patrese	'99	R. Barrichello
'92	N. Mansell	'00	M. Schumacher
'93	D. Hill	'01	R. Schumacher
'94	D. Hill	'02	J.P. Montoya
'95	D. Hill	'03	R. Schumacher
'96	M. Schumacher	'04	F. Alonso
'97	M. Schumacher	'05	F. Alonso

	1°	2°	3°
'90	A. Prost	I. Capelli	A. Senna
'91	N. Mansell	A. Prost	A. Senna
'92	N. Mansell	A. Prost	M. Brundle
'93	A. Prost	D. Hill	M. Schumacher
'94	M. Schumacher	D. Hill	G. Berger
'95	M. Schumacher	D. Hill	D. Coulthard
'96	D. Hill	J. Villeneuve	J. Alesi
'97	M. Schumacher	H.H. Frentzen	E. Irvine
'98	M. Schumacher	E. Irvine	M. Hakkinen
'99	H.H. Frentzen	M. Hakkinen	R. Barrichello
'00	D. Coulthard	M. Hakkinen	R. Barrichello
'01	M. Schumacher	R. Schumacher	R. Barrichello
'02	M. Schumacher	K. Raikkonen	D. Coulthard
'03	R. Schumacher	J.P. Montoya	M. Schumacher
'04	M. Schumacher	F. Alonso	R. Barrichello

STARTING GRID

1 FERNANDO ALONSO — RENAULT / JARNO TRULLI — TOYOTA

2 MICHAEL SCHUMACHER — FERRARI / TAKUMA SATO — BAR

3 RUBENS BARRICHELLO — FERRARI / GIANCARLO FISICHELLA — RENAULT

4 JENSON BUTTON — BAR / JUAN PABLO MONTOYA — MCLAREN

5 FELIPE MASSA — SAUBER / JACQUES VILLENEUVE — SAUBER

6 RALF SCHUMACHER — TOYOTA / MARK WEBBER — WILLIAMS

7 KIMI RAIKKONEN — MCLAREN / NICK HEIDFELD — WILLIAMS

8 DAVID COULTHARD — RED BULL / CHRISTIAN KLIEN — RED BULL

9 NARAIN KARTHIKEYAN — JORDAN / PATRICK FRIESACHER — MINARDI

10 TIAGO MONTEIRO — JORDAN / CHRISTIJAN ALBERS — MINARDI

RESULTS

	DRIVER	CAR	KPH	GAP
1	F. Alonso	Renault	202,638	-
2	K. Raikkonen	McLaren	202,202	0'11"805
3	M. Schumacher	Ferrari	199,654	1'21"914
4	J. Button	BAR	199,605	1 lap
5	J. Trulli	Toyota	199,444	1 lap
6	G. Fisichella	Renault	199,122	1 lap
7	R. Schumacher	Toyota	198,650	1 lap
8	J. Villeneuve	Sauber	198,494	1 lap
9	R. Barrichello	Ferrari	198,360	1 lap
10	D. Coulthard	Red Bull	198,278	1 lap
11	T. Sato	BAR	197,576	1 lap
12	M. Webber	Williams	196,330	2 laps
13	T. Monteiro	Jordan	192,404	3 laps
14	N. Heidfeld	Williams	189,564	4 laps
15	N. Karthikeyan	Jordan	189,409	4 laps

RETIREMENTS

J.P. Montoya	McLaren	46	Hydraulic circuit
C. Albers	Minardi	37	Wheel
P. Friesacher	Minardi	33	Wheel
F. Massa	Sauber	30	Hydraulic circuit
C. Klien	Red Bull	1	Fuel pressure

THE RACE

DRIVER	CAR	LAP	FASTEST LAP	TOP SPEED
K. Raikkonen	McLaren	25	1'16"423	321,6
F. Alonso	Renault	5	1'16"502	318,8
J.P. Montoya	McLaren	24	1'16"656	319,5
J. Button	BAR	18	1'17"408	319,9
G. Fisichella	Renault	18	1'17"511	319,3
D. Coulthard	Red Bull	39	1'17"611	320,0
M. Schumacher	Ferrari	22	1'17"714	317,6
J. Trulli	Toyota	67	1'17"792	314,2
F. Massa	Sauber	11	1'17"805	315,1
J. Villeneuve	Sauber	17	1'17"841	315,4
T. Sato	BAR	8	1'17"929	321,0
R. Barrichello	Ferrari	4	1'17"960	319,1
N. Heidfeld	Williams	36	1'18"102	313,6
R. Schumacher	Toyota	36	1'18"103	318,3
M. Webber	Williams	17	1'18"395	313,2
T. Monteiro	Jordan	32	1'20"004	312,6
N. Karthikeyan	Jordan	9	1'20"156	314,5
C. Albers	Minardi	8	1'21"077	322,0
P. Friesacher	Minardi	4	1'21"451	317,7
C. Klien	Red Bull	-	-	-

FRENCH GP

HOME WIN FOR RENAULT

The presence of Renault boss Carlos Ghosn, who is not exactly in favour of the French manufacturer's participation in Formula 1 due to the high costs involved, seemed to give Briatore's team the horsepower and the determination required at their home circuit to convince him otherwise.

And the Renault team certainly did its part at Magny-Cours. Alonso immediately set pole position in qualifying and Fisichella sixth quickest time, while Trulli was second on the grid for Toyota, followed by Schumacher and Takuma Sato. Raikkonen was furious after losing ten positions due to yet another engine failure in Friday practice.

Alonso powered away at the start and began to reel off a series of quick laps in which he pulled out a comfortable lead over his rivals. Raikkonen, who had started with a heavy fuel load in view of a two-stop strategy, began his recovery and moved through the field.

Ralf Schumacher and Villeneuve were first to succumb to the Finn's attacks, while the others had to make an extra pit-stop as the McLaren stayed out on the track.

At the chequered flag Raikkonen finished an excellent runner-up, limiting the damage caused by his poor starting grid position.

Third went to Schumacher, who ran an honest race but the German could do little else but hold off his closest rivals, who were Button, Trulli and Fisichella in that order.

Renault's Italian driver was turning into a sort of Barrichello of recent years, always claiming that his car was having problems and that the team were doing their best to penalise him.

This time in the race he had a problem with his Renault's flat bottom and then he came in for a never-ending first pit stop and in the second his engine stalled, but it was apparently not his fault.

In the same unfortunate company as Fisichella was McLaren's Colombian driver Montoya, who ran second for a number of laps and who was forced to retire once again with a problem in the hydraulic system.

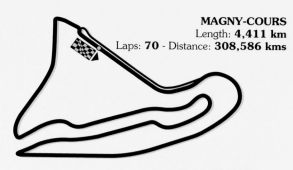

What's the quickest car on the track? It might seem incredible but it was the Minardi, which with Albers behind the wheel, reached a top speed of 322 km/h in the race, almost 10 km/h quicker than the Williams, which was the slowest.
A prize must surely go to Minardi's aerodynamics designers, who despite a limited budget and an engine that has seen better days, have clearly managed to create an excellent car.

The entire Renault top brass were out in force in the French team's pit garage at their home circuit. And Fernando Alonso didn't disappoint them as he powered to pole position and took the win over his chief rival Raikkonen.

	CHAMPIONSHIPS POINTS	AUSTRALIAN GP	MALAYSIAN GP	BAHRAIN GP	SAN MARINO GP	SPANISH GP	MONACO GP	EUROPEAN GP	CANADIAN GP	UNITED STATES GP	FRENCH GP	BRITISH GP	GERMAN GP	HUNGARIAN GP	TURKISH GP	ITALIAN GP	BELGIUM GP	BRAZILIAN GP	JAPANESE GP	CHINA GP	TOTAL POINT
1	F. ALONSO	6	10	10	10	8	5	10	-	rit.	10										69
2	K. RAIKKONEN	1	-	6	-	10	10	-	10	rit.	8										45
3	M. SCHUMACHER	-	2	-	8	-	2	4	8	10	6										40
4	J. TRULLI	-	8	8	4	6	-	1	-	rit.	4										31
5	R. BARRICHELLO	8	-	-	-	-	1	6	6	8	-										29
6	N. HEIDFELD	-	6	-	3	-	8	8	-	rit.	-										25
7	M. WEBBER	4	-	3	2	3	6	-	4	rit.	-										22
8	R. SCHUMACHER	-	4	5	-	5	3	-	3	rit.	2										22
9	G. FISICHELLA	10	-	-	-	4	-	3	-	rit.	3										20
10	D. COULTHARD	5	3	1	-	1	-	5	2	rit.	-										17
11	J.P. MONTOYA	3	5	/	/	2	4	2	sq.	rit.	-										16
12	F. MASSA	-	-	2	-	-	-	-	-	5	rit.										7
13	T. MONTEIRO	-	-	-	-	-	-	-	-	6	-										6
14	A. WURZ	/	/	/	6	/	/	/	/	/	/										6
15	J. VILLENEUVE	-	-	-	5	-	-	-	-	rit.	1										6
16	J. BUTTON	-	-	-	sq.	sq.	sq.	-	-	rit.	5										5
17	N. KARTHIKEYAN	-	-	-	-	-	-	-	-	5	-										5
18	C. ALBERS	-	-	-	-	-	-	-	-	4	-										4
19	P. DE LA ROSA	/	/	4	/	/	/	/	/	/	/										4
20	C. KLIEN	2	1	-	/	/	-	-	1	rit.	-										4
21	P. FRIESACHER	-	-	-	-	-	-	-	-	3	-										3
22	V. LIUZZI	/	/	/	1	-	-	-	-	/	/										1
23	T. SATO	-	-	-	sq.	sq.	sq.	-	-	rit.	-										0
24	A. DAVIDSON	/	-	/	/	/	/	/	/	/	/										0

rit.: Retired   **sq.:** Disqualified

SILVERSTONE
10 JULY 2005

POLE POSITION

STARTING GRID

1
 FERNANDO ALONSO — RENAULT
 JENSON BUTTON — BAR

2
 JUAN PABLO MONTOYA — MCLAREN
 JARNO TRULLI — TOYOTA

3
 RUBENS BARRICHELLO — FERRARI
 GIANCARLO FISICHELLA — RENAULT

4
 TAKUMA SATO — BAR
 RALF SCHUMACHER — TOYOTA

5
 MICHAEL SCHUMACHER — FERRARI
 JACQUES VILLENEUVE — SAUBER

6
 MARK WEBBER — WILLIAMS
 KIMI RAIKKONEN — MCLAREN

7
 DAVID COULTHARD — RED BULL
 NICK HEIDFELD — WILLIAMS

8
 CHRISTIAN KLIEN — RED BULL
 FELIPE MASSA — SAUBER

9
 NARAIN KARTHIKEYAN — JORDAN
 CHRISTIJAN ALBERS — MINARDI

10
 PATRICK FRIESACHER — MINARDI
 TIAGO MONTEIRO — JORDAN

RESULTS

	DRIVER	CAR	KPH	GAP
1	J.P. Montoya	McLaren	218,968	-
2	F. Alonso	Renault	218,849	0'02"739
3	K. Raikkonen	McLaren	218,346	0'14"436
4	G. Fisichella	Renault	218,197	0'17"914
5	J. Button	BAR	217,242	0'40"264
6	M. Schumacher	Ferrari	215,762	1'15"322
7	R. Barrichello	Ferrari	215,710	1'16"567
8	R. Schumacher	Toyota	215,599	1'19"212
9	J. Trulli	Toyota	215,530	1'20"851
10	F. Massa	Sauber	214,396	1 lap
11	M. Webber	Williams	212,932	1 lap
12	N. Heidfeld	Williams	212,671	1 lap
13	D. Coulthard	Red Bull	212,636	1 lap
14	J. Villeneuve	Sauber	212,510	1 lap
15	C. Klien	Red Bull	212,482	1 lap
16	T. Sato	BAR	209,494	2 laps
17	T. Monteiro	Jordan	208,277	2 laps
18	C. Albers	Minardi	205,998	3 laps
19	P. Friesacher	Minardi	203,893	4 laps

RETIREMENTS

N. Karthikeyan	Jordan	10	Electrical

THE RACE

DRIVER	CAR	LAP	FASTEST LAP	TOP SPEED
K. Raikkonen	McLaren	60	1'20"502	278,2
J.P. Montoya	McLaren	41	1'20"700	278,4
G. Fisichella	Renault	43	1'21"159	280,6
F. Alonso	Renault	40	1'21"228	283,2
M. Schumacher	Ferrari	23	1'21"675	273,1
R. Schumacher	Toyota	46	1'21"960	286,1
J. Button	BAR	42	1'21"993	280,0
J. Trulli	Toyota	56	1'22"112	282,2
R. Barrichello	Ferrari	41	1'22"302	269,4
F. Massa	Sauber	45	1'22"466	273,7
T. Sato	BAR	54	1'22"551	276,4
D. Coulthard	Red Bull	44	1'23"089	268,9
C. Klien	Red Bull	58	1'23"147	275,2
J. Villeneuve	Sauber	16	1'23"210	267,0
M. Webber	Williams	16	1'23"291	279,4
N. Heidfeld	Williams	58	1'23"360	276,0
T. Monteiro	Jordan	38	1'24"247	267,5
N. Karthikeyan	Jordan	8	1'25"257	254,6
C. Albers	Minardi	53	1'26"182	253,5
P. Friesacher	Minardi	37	1'26"489	260,6

BRITISH GP

McLaren and Montoya: From Dust to Stardust

Fernando Alonso powered to another pole at Silverstone
and the Spaniard was flanked on the grid by Jenson Button and followed
on row 2 by Juan Pablo Montoya and Jarno Trulli.

Raikkonen was once again penalized ten positions for an engine
change after setting second quickest time in qualifying.

Things looked to be going Renault's way once again because the French
cars were known for their superb launch control system, but Montoya occasionally
remembers he is a top-class Formula 1 driver and at the first corner he overtook
Button, powered alongside Alonso and took the lead of the race.

The Silverstone GP was a two-way battle between these drivers.

It was decided by pit-stop strategies but also by the overtaking moves
carried out on the back-markers with great determination by the Colombian
and with a bit more circumspection by Alonso, who was just intent
on finishing and bringing home the points.

Raikkonen, who started down the grid, could also have been
in the hunt for the win, because he drove an outstanding race and powered
his way through the field to finish in third place.

For the joy of Ron Dennis, the race finished with two McLarens
on the podium, but Flavio Briatore was also satisfied with Alonso's second
place and a fourth place for Fisichella, who again had problems
at Silverstone when he stalled during the pit stop.

The Italian maintained it was a problem with the electronics
but Briatore put the blame on the driver.

The fact remains that for Fisichella the podium was once again
a mere illusion and his win in Australia a flash in the pan.

Twenty cars started the British GP and nineteen finished. The only retirement was Karthikeyan in the Jordan, who went out with an electronics problem. This was a demonstration of the incredible reliability reached by the engines of modern-day Formula 1 cars, despite the fact that they are obliged to last for two successive races, with a ten-place grid penalty should they fail to comply. To be honest, the Mercedes still has a few problems, as demonstrated by Raikkonen, who is constantly forced to produce some stunning drives just to get into the top positions.

After a Renault win in France, a McLaren win in Britain would have been a fair result. And so it was, only that with the championship in mind, it was the wrong driver. Montoya in fact took the win, followed by Alonso, with Raikkonen only managing third.

	CHAMPIONSHIPS POINTS	AUSTRALIAN GP	MALAYSIAN GP	BAHRAIN GP	SAN MARINO GP	SPANISH GP	MONACO GP	EUROPEAN GP	CANADIAN GP	UNITED STATES GP	FRENCH GP	BRITISH GP	GERMAN GP	HUNGARIAN GP	TURKISH GP	ITALIAN GP	BELGIUM GP	BRAZILIAN GP	JAPANESE GP	CHINA GP	TOTAL POINT
1	F. ALONSO	6	10	10	10	8	5	10	-	rit.	10	8									77
2	K. RAIKKONEN	1	-	6	-	10	10	-	10	rit.	8	6									51
3	M. SCHUMACHER	-	2	-	8	-	2	4	8	10	6	3									43
4	J. TRULLI	-	8	8	4	6	-	1	-	rit.	4	-									31
5	R. BARRICHELLO	8	-	-	-	-	1	6	6	8	-	2									31
6	J.P. MONTOYA	3	5	/	/	2	4	2	sq.	rit.	-	10									26
7	G. FISICHELLA	10	-	-	-	4	-	3	-	rit.	3	5									25
8	N. HEIDFELD	-	6	-	3	-	8	8	-	rit.	-	-									25
9	R. SCHUMACHER	-	4	5	-	5	3	-	3	rit.	2	1									23
10	M. WEBBER	4	-	3	2	3	6	-	4	rit.	-	-									22
11	D. COULTHARD	5	3	1	-	1	-	5	2	rit.	-	-									17
12	J. BUTTON	-	-	-	sq.	sq.	sq.	-	-	rit.	5	4									9
13	F. MASSA	-	-	2	-	-	-	-	5	rit.	-	-									7
14	T. MONTEIRO	-	-	-	-	-	-	-	-	6	-	-									6
15	A. WURZ	/	/	/	6	/	/	/	/	/	/	/									6
16	J. VILLENEUVE	-	-	-	5	-	-	-	-	rit.	1	-									6
17	N. KARTHIKEYAN	-	-	-	-	-	-	-	-	5	-	-									5
18	C. ALBERS	-	-	-	-	-	-	-	-	4	-	-									4
19	P. DE LA ROSA	/	/	4	/	/	/	/	/	/	/	/									4
20	C. KLIEN	2	1	-	/	/	/	/	1	rit.	-	-									4
21	P. FRIESACHER	-	-	-	-	-	-	-	-	3	-	-									3
22	V. LIUZZI	/	/	/	1	-	-	-	-	/	/	/									1
23	T. SATO	-	-	-	sq.	sq.	sq.	-	-	rit.	-	-									0
24	A. DAVIDSON	-	-	/	/	/	/	/	-	/	/	/									0

rit.: Retired   **sq.:** Disqualified

POLE POSITION

'90	A. Senna	'98	M. Hakkinen
'91	N. Mansell	'99	M. Hakkinen
'92	N. Mansell	'00	D. Coulthard
'93	A. Prost	'01	J.P. Montoya
'94	G. Berger	'02	M. Schumacher
'95	D. Hill	'03	J.P. Montoya
'96	D. Hill	'04	M. Schumacher
'97	G. Berger	'05	K. Raikkonen

	1°	2°	3°
'90	A. Senna	A. Nannini	G. Berger
'91	N. Mansell	R. Patrese	J. Alesi
'92	N. Mansell	A. Senna	M. Schumacher
'93	A. Prost	M. Schumacher	M. Brundell
'94	G. Berger	O. Panis	E. Bernard
'95	M. Schumacher	D. Coulthard	G. Berger
'96	D. Hill	J. Alesi	J. Villeneuve
'97	G. Berger	M. Schumacher	M. Hakkinen
'98	M. Hakkinen	D. Coulthard	J. Villeneuve
'99	E. Irvine	M. Salo	H.H. Frentzen
'00	R. Barrichello	M. Hakkinen	D. Coulthard
'01	R. Schumacher	R. Barrichello	J. Villeneuve
'02	M. Schumacher	J.P. Montoya	R. Schumacher
'03	J.P. Montoya	D. Coulthard	J. Trulli
'04	M. Schumacher	J. Button	F. Alonso

STARTING GRID

1 — KIMI RAIKKONEN — McLAREN | JENSON BUTTON — BAR

2 — FERNANDO ALONSO — RENAULT | GIANCARLO FISICHELLA — RENAULT

3 — MICHAEL SCHUMACHER — FERRARI | MARK WEBBER — WILLIAMS

4 — NICK HEIDFELD — WILLIAMS | TAKUMA SATO — BAR

5 — JARNO TRULLI — TOYOTA | CHRISTIAN KLIEN — RED BULL

6 — DAVID COULTHARD — RED BULL | RALF SCHUMACHER — TOYOTA

7 — FELIPE MASSA — SAUBER | JACQUES VILLENEUVE — SAUBER

8 — RUBENS BARRICHELLO — FERRARI | CHRISTIJAN ALBERS — MINARDI

9 — ROBERT DOORNBOS — MINARDI | TIAGO MONTEIRO — JORDAN

10 — NARAIN KARTHIKEYAN — JORDAN | JUAN PABLO MONTOYA — McLAREN

RESULTS

	DRIVER	CAR	KPH	GAP
1	F. Alonso	Renault	212,629	-
2	J.P. Montoya	McLaren	211,708	0'22"569
3	J. Button	BAR	211,633	0'24"422
4	G. Fisichella	Renault	210,576	0'50"587
5	M. Schumacher	Ferrari	210,532	0'51"690
6	R. Schumacher	Toyota	210,509	0'52"242
7	D. Coulthard	Red Bull	210,491	0'52"700
8	F. Massa	Sauber	210,336	0'56"570
9	C. Klien	Red Bull	209,806	1'09"818
10	R. Barrichello	Ferrari	209,184	1 lap
11	N. Heidfeld	Williams	208,168	1 lap
12	T. Sato	BAR	208,037	1 lap
13	C. Albers	Minardi	203,401	2 laps
14	J. Villeneuve	Sauber	202,264	3 laps
15	N. Karthikeyan	Jordan	200,432	3 laps
16	T. Monteiro	Jordan	200,244	3 laps
17	R. Doornbos	Minardi	199,433	4 laps

RETIREMENTS

J. Trulli	Toyota	64	Engine
M. Webber	Williams	55	Not classified
K. Raikkonen	McLaren	35	Hydraulic circuit

THE RACE

DRIVER	CAR	LAP	FASTEST LAP	TOP SPEED
K. Raikkonen	McLaren	24	1'14"873	327,1
F. Alonso	Renault	21	1'15"235	328,2
J. Button	BAR	19	1'15"843	326,5
J.P. Montoya	McLaren	54	1'15"878	341,0
G. Fisichella	Renault	21	1'15"890	330,5
R. Schumacher	Toyota	23	1'16"073	329,9
M. Schumacher	Ferrari	18	1'16"099	323,9
D. Coulthard	Red Bull	18	1'16"233	329,6
C. Klien	Red Bull	45	1'16"236	329,4
F. Massa	Sauber	45	1'16"288	327,6
J. Trulli	Toyota	45	1'16"474	329,8
R. Barrichello	Ferrari	47	1'16"528	321,4
N. Heidfeld	Williams	10	1'16"607	323,4
T. Sato	BAR	27	1'16"725	324,6
M. Webber	Williams	46	1'16"803	314,7
J. Villeneuve	Sauber	26	1'17"122	331,4
T. Monteiro	Jordan	12	1'18"106	323,0
N. Karthikeyan	Jordan	7	1'18"212	323,9
C. Albers	Minardi	11	1'18"425	330,1
R. Doornbos	Minardi	44	1'19"025	324,5

German GP

HOCKENHEIM
Length: **4,574 km**
Laps: **67** - Distance: **306,458 kms**

McLaren Self Destruct

Both McLarens could easily have been on the front row of the grid
for the start of the German GP but in qualifying Montoya ruined an excellent
quick lap by going off the circuit at the final curve before the finish line.
The Colombian's car was destroyed and he was relegated to the back of the grid,
while Raikkonen kept the pole. The Finn found Button alongside in the BAR,
with the two Renaults menacingly on the second row.

The two Minardis produced a good performance in qualifying with Albers
and first-timer Doornbos, who were ahead of the two Jordans.

Both McLarens could easily also have made the podium, had Raikkonen
not come to a halt half-way through the race when something nasty happened
in the hydraulics system and it lost all of its oil.

This was just another chapter in a championship that has now probably
been lost by McLaren, despite the Anglo-German team having an extraordinary
driver and a fantastic car. Unfortunately the McLarens often seem to encounter a
series of electronics or engine problems and even carelessness
by the team has lent a helping hand.

Luckily Montoya managed to bring home eight precious points by finishing
second, despite starting the race from the final grid position.

Button also produced an excellent performance to take his first podium finish
of the year, if one excludes the result at Imola when he was disqualified. Jenson's
move on Schumacher at the end of the race, when the German was in all sorts
of tyre trouble and had been passed by Fisichella, was a superb one.

Raikkonen left the circuit without making any statements, furious over yet another
retirement when he had the race in the bag, while Briatore was coming closer
and closer to a title that he had so confidently predicted one year before.

Two Dutch drivers certainly represents something
new in Formula 1. Christijan Albers was in fact joined
by the 24-year-old Formula 3000 driver,
Robert Doornbos from Rotterdam.
The last Dutchman in Formula 1 was Jos Verstappen,
who also drove for Minardi, in the 2003 season.

Alonso celebrated his sixth win of the year
and Raikkonen blamed sheer misfortune as he
was forced into retirement half-way through the
race with a hydraulic failure. The only satisfaction
for McLaren was Montoya's second place.

	CHAMPIONSHIPS POINTS	AUSTRALIAN GP	MALAYSIAN GP	BAHRAIN GP	SAN MARINO GP	SPANISH GP	MONACO GP	EUROPEAN GP	CANADIAN GP	UNITED STATES GP	FRENCH GP	BRITISH GP	GERMAN GP	HUNGARIAN GP	TURKISH GP	ITALIAN GP	BELGIUM GP	BRAZILIAN GP	JAPANESE GP	CHINA GP	TOTAL POINT
1	F. ALONSO	6	10	10	10	8	5	10	-	rit.	10	8	10								87
2	K. RAIKKONEN	1	-	6	-	10	10	-	10	rit.	8	6	-								51
3	M. SCHUMACHER	-	2	-	8	-	2	4	8	10	6	3	4								47
4	J.P. MONTOYA	3	5	/	/	2	4	2	sq.	rit.	-	10	8								34
5	R. BARRICHELLO	8	-	-	-	-	1	6	6	8	-	2	-								31
6	J. TRULLI	-	8	8	4	6	-	1	-	rit.	4	-	-								31
7	G. FISICHELLA	10	-	-	-	4	-	3	-	rit.	3	5	5								30
8	R. SCHUMACHER	-	4	5	-	5	3	-	3	rit.	2	1	3								26
9	N. HEIDFELD	-	6	-	3	-	8	8	-	rit.	-	-	-								25
10	M. WEBBER	4	-	3	2	3	6	-	4	rit.	-	-	-								22
11	D. COULTHARD	5	3	1	-	1	-	5	2	rit.	-	-	2								19
12	J. BUTTON	-	-	sq.	sq.	sq.	-	-	-	rit.	5	4	6								15
13	F. MASSA	-	-	2	-	-	-	-	5	rit.	-	-	1								8
14	T. MONTEIRO	-	-	-	-	-	-	-	-	6	-	-	-								6
15	A. WURZ	/	/	/	6	/	/	/	/	/	/	/	/								6
16	J. VILLENEUVE	-	-	-	5	-	-	-	-	rit.	1	-	-								6
17	N. KARTHIKEYAN	-	-	-	-	-	-	-	-	5	-	-	-								5
18	C. ALBERS	-	-	-	-	-	-	-	-	4	-	-	-								4
19	P. DE LA ROSA	/	/	4	/	/	/	/	/	/	/	/	/								4
20	C. KLIEN	2	1	-	/	/	/	/	1	rit.	-	-	-								4
21	P. FRIESACHER	-	-	-	-	-	-	-	-	3	/	/	/								3
22	V. LIUZZI	/	/	/	1	-	-	-	/	/	/	/	/								1
23	T. SATO	-	-	-	sq.	sq.	sq.	-	-	rit.	-	-	-								0
24	A. DAVIDSON	/	-	/	/	/	/	/	/	/	/	/	/								0
25	R. DOORNBOS	/	/	/	/	/	/	/	/	/	/	/	-								0

rit.: Retired   **sq.**: Disqualified

POLE POSITION

'90	T. Boutsen		'98	M. Hakkinen
'91	A. Senna		'99	M. Hakkinen
'92	R. Patrese		'00	M. Schumacher
'93	A. Prost		'01	M. Schumacher
'94	M. Schumacher		'02	R. Barrichello
'95	D. Hill		'03	F. Alonso
'96	M. Schumacher		'04	M. Schumacher
'97	M. Schumacher		'05	M. Schumacher

STARTING GRID

1
 MICHAEL SCHUMACHER — FERRARI
 JUAN PABLO MONTOYA — MCLAREN

2
 JARNO TRULLI — TOYOTA
 KIMI RAIKKONEN — MCLAREN

3
 RALF SCHUMACHER — TOYOTA
 FERNANDO ALONSO — RENAULT

4
 RUBENS BARRICHELLO — FERRARI
 JENSON BUTTON — BAR

5
 GIANCARLO FISICHELLA — RENAULT
 TAKUMA SATO — BAR

6
 CHRISTIAN KLIEN — RED BULL
 NICK HEIDFELD — WILLIAMS

7
 DAVID COULTHARD — RED BULL
 FELIPE MASSA — SAUBER

8
 JACQUES VILLENEUVE — SAUBER
 MARK WEBBER — WILLIAMS

9
 CHRISTIJAN ALBERS — MINARDI
 NARAIN KARTHIKEYAN — JORDAN

10
 ROBERT DOORNBOS — MINARDI
 TIAGO MONTEIRO — JORDAN

		1°	2°	3°
'90		T. Boutsen	A. Senna	N. Piquet
'91		A. Senna	N. Mansell	R. Patrese
'92		A. Senna	N. Mansell	G. Berger
'93		D. Hill	R. Patrese	G. Berger
'94		M. Schumacher	D. Hill	J. Verstappen
'95		D. Hill	D. Coulthard	G. Berger
'96		J. Villeneuve	D. Hill	J. Alesi
'97		J. Villeneuve	D. Hill	J. Herbert
'98		M. Schumacher	D. Coulthard	J. Villeneuve
'99		M. Hakkinen	D. Coulthard	E. Irvine
'00		M. Hakkinen	M. Schumacher	D. Coulthard
'01		M. Schumacher	R. Barrichello	D. Coulthard
'02		R. Barrichello	M. Schumacher	R. Schumacher
'03		F. Alonso	K. Raikkonen	J.P. Montoya
'04		M. Schumacher	R. Barrichello	F. Alonso

RESULTS

	DRIVER	CAR	KPH	GAP
1	K. Raikkonen	McLaren	188,859	-
2	M. Schumacher	Ferrari	187,716	0'35"581
3	R. Schumacher	Toyota	187,699	0'36"129
4	J. Trulli	Toyota	187,123	0'54"221
5	J. Button	BAR	186,977	0'58"832
6	N. Heidfeld	Williams	186,675	1'08"375
7	M. Webber	Williams	185,914	1 lap
8	T. Sato	BAR	185,497	1 lap
9	G. Fisichella	Renault	184,841	1 lap
10	R. Barrichello	Ferrari	184,623	1 lap
11	F. Alonso	Renault	184,585	1 lap
12	N. Karthikeyan	Jordan	179,388	3 laps
13	T. Monteiro	Jordan	176,832	4 laps
14	F. Massa	Sauber	167,867	7 laps

RETIREMENTS

C. Albers	Minardi	59	Hydraulic circuit
J. Villeneuve	Sauber	56	Electrical
J.P. Montoya	McLaren	41	Axle-shaft
R. Doornbos	Minardi	26	Hydraulic circuit
C. Klien	Red Bull	0	Accident
D. Coulthard	Red Bull	0	Accident

THE RACE

DRIVER	CAR	LAP	FASTEST LAP	TOP SPEED
K. Raikkonen	McLaren	40	1'21"219	309,2
J.P. Montoya	McLaren	20	1'21"237	309,3
M. Schumacher	Ferrari	13	1'21"476	303,7
J. Trulli	Toyota	32	1'21"842	301,9
R. Schumacher	Toyota	13	1'21"873	302,9
N. Heidfeld	Williams	53	1'22"053	302,7
T. Sato	BAR	45	1'22"399	305,3
J. Button	BAR	70	1'22"406	306,1
M. Webber	Williams	47	1'22"453	309,5
G. Fisichella	Renault	19	1'22"506	306,9
R. Barrichello	Ferrari	20	1'22"768	308,8
F. Alonso	Renault	51	1'22"884	306,9
F. Massa	Sauber	22	1'23"048	301,5
J. Villeneuve	Sauber	23	1'23"118	305,4
N. Karthikeyan	Jordan	17	1'24"446	300,7
T. Monteiro	Jordan	15	1'24"774	302,6
R. Doornbos	Minardi	16	1'25"646	301,8
C. Albers	Minardi	8	1'25"956	301,1
D. Coulthard	Red Bull	-	-	-
C. Klien	Red Bull	-	-	-

HUNGARIAN GP

HUNGARORING
Length:
4,381 km
Laps: **70**
Distance:
306,663 kms

SCHUMACHER'S FLASH OF PRIDE

Schumacher demonstrated all of his class and experience at this medium-slow circuit where tyre problems would be considerably reduced. The German finally set his first pole position of the year, almost one second ahead of Montoya, Trulli, Raikkonen and brother Ralf.

It was strange to see the two Renaults in difficulty on a circuit where they were thought to have a considerable traction advantage.

At the first corner bottleneck following the start, Alonso made contact with Ralf Schumacher, damaging the nose of his Renault, while right behind, Klien in the Red Bull was involved in a spectacular crash in which he overturned after making contact with Villeneuve (Sauber).

It was a GP to forget for Red Bull, which in the space of the same lap also lost Coulthard, who collected Alonso's detached front wing and damaged his front suspension.

Following the chaos of the start it was Montoya who took the lead of the race and the Colombian stayed there until well over half-distance before retiring with a broken driveshaft, possibly the result of him making contact with a BAR generator while the cars were lining up on the grid.

Schumacher inherited the lead of the race followed by Raikkonen, who was simply unable to pass despite having the superior car.

The Finn was only able to do so because of a better pit stop strategy and the fact that he could accumulate an advantage on the track while the Ferrari driver pitted.

Raikkonen went on to take the chequered flag for the ten points, while Alonso failed to notch up a single point as he could only finish ninth.

Second place went to Michael Schumacher, followed by his brother Ralf, who scored his first podium with the Toyota, and Trulli.

The gap between the two young chargers at the top of the table was now 26 points, with six rounds left.

Alonso still had a big lead but in the last few races the McLarens, despite a few reliability problems, were demonstrating that they were back at the top while Raikkonen was becoming more and more confident as the season progressed.

HIGHLIGHTS

Right from the very start, the Hungarian GP has always been considered by the Finns to be their 'home' race. This was because it coincides with their traditional holiday period and also because it is their closest race to home. This year the number of Finnish fans was greater than usual and they included one VIP: Mika Hakkinen, the two-times world champion (1998/1999), who had come to see his old friends at McLaren and cheer on his pupil Raikkonen. And his presence was felt!

PHOTO PORTFOLIO

Finally a pole position for Schumacher and smiles on the face of the Ferrari clan after a season of disappointment. The race win however went to Raikkonen for the fourth time this year, while the other two podium positions went to the two Schumacher brothers, with Ralf scoring his first podium of the year.

CHAMPIONSHIPS POINTS	Australian GP	Malaysian GP	Bahrain GP	San Marino GP	Spanish GP	Monaco GP	European GP	Canadian GP	United States GP	French GP	British GP	German GP	Hungarian GP	Turkish GP	Italian GP	Belgium GP	Brazilian GP	Japanese GP	China GP	TOTAL POINT
1 F. ALONSO	6	10	10	10	8	5	10	-	rit.	10	8	10	-							87
2 K. RAIKKONEN	1	-	6	-	10	10	-	10	rit.	8	6	-	10							61
3 M. SCHUMACHER	-	2	-	8	-	2	4	8	10	6	3	4	8							55
4 J. TRULLI	-	8	8	4	6	-	1	-	4	-	-	-	5							36
5 J.P. MONTOYA	3	5	/		2	4	2	sq.	rit.	-	10	8								34
6 R. SCHUMACHER	-	4	5	-	5	3	-	3	rit.	2	1	3	6							32
7 R. BARRICHELLO	8	-	-		-	1	6	6	8	-	2	-	-							31
8 G. FISICHELLA	10	-	-		4	-		3	rit.	3	5	5	-							30
9 N. HEIDFELD	-	6	-	3	-	8	8	-	rit.	-	-	-	3							28
10 M. WEBBER	4	-	3	2	3	6	-	4	rit.	-	-	-	2							24
11 D. COULTHARD	5	3	1	-	1	-	5	2	rit.	-	-	2	-							19
12 J. BUTTON	-	-	-	sq.	sq.	sq.	-	-	rit.	5	4	6	4							19
13 F. MASSA	-	-	2	-	-	-	-	5	rit.	-	1	-	-							8
14 T. MONTEIRO	-	-	-	-	-	-	-	-	6	-	-	-	-							6
15 A. WURZ	/	/	/	6	/	/	/	/	/	/	/	/	/							6
16 J. VILLENEUVE	-	-	-	5	-	-	-	-	rit.	1	-	-	-							6
17 N. KARTHIKEYAN	-	-	-	-	-	-	-	-	5	-	-	-	-							5
18 C. ALBERS	-	-	-	-	-	-	-	-	4	-	-	-	-							4
19 P. DE LA ROSA	/	/	4	/	/	/	/	/	/	/	/	/	/							4
20 C. KLIEN	2	1	-	/	/	/	/	1	rit.	-	-	-	-							4
21 P. FRIESACHER	-	-	-	-	-	-	-	-	3	-	-	-	-							3
22 V. LIUZZI	-	-	-	-	1	-	-	-	-	/	/	/	/							1
23 T. SATO	-	-	-	sq.	sq.	sq.	-	-	rit.	-	-	-	1							1
24 A. DAVIDSON	/	-	/	/	/	/	/	/	/	/	/	-	-							0
25 R. DOORNBOS	/	/	/	/	/	/	/	/	/	/	/	-	-							0

rit.: Retired   **sq.:** Disqualified

POLE POSITION

STARTING GRID

1

KIMI RAIKKONEN
MCLAREN

GIANCARLO FISICHELLA
RENAULT

2

FERNANDO ALONSO
RENAULT

JUAN PABLO MONTOYA
MCLAREN

3

JARNO TRULLI
TOYOTA

NICK HEIDFELD
WILLIAMS

4

MARK WEBBER
WILLIAMS

FELIPE MASSA
SAUBER

5

RALF SCHUMACHER
TOYOTA

CHRISTIAN KLIEN
RED BULL

6

RUBENS BARRICHELLO
FERRARI

DAVID COULTHARD
RED BULL

7

JENSON BUTTON
BAR

TIAGO MONTEIRO
JORDAN

8

CHRISTIJAN ALBERS
MINARDI

JACQUES VILLENEUVE
SAUBER

9

ROBERT DOORNBOS
MINARDI

NARAIN KARTHIKEYAN
JORDAN

10

MICHAEL SCHUMACHER
FERRARI

TAKUMA SATO
BAR

RESULTS

	DRIVER	CAR	KPH	GAP
1	K. Raikkonen	McLaren	219,496	-
2	F. Alonso	Renault	218,694	0'18"609
3	J.P. Montoya	McLaren	218,650	0'19"635
4	G. Fisichella	Renault	217,866	0'37"973
5	J. Button	BAR	217,809	0'39"304
6	J. Trulli	Toyota	217,125	0'55"420
7	D. Coulthard	Red Bull	216,539	1'09"296
8	C. Klien	Red Bull	216,441	1'11"622
9	T. Sato	BAR	214,840	1'49"987
10	R. Barrichello	Ferrari	215,581	1 lap
11	J. Villeneuve	Sauber	214,291	1 lap
12	R. Schumacher	Toyota	214,267	1 lap
13	R. Doornbos	Minardi	207,543	3 laps
14	N. Karthikeyan	Jordan	207,030	3 laps
15	T. Monteiro	Jordan	206,482	3 laps

RETIREMENTS

C. Albers	Minardi	48	Gearbox
M. Schumacher	Ferrari	32	Accident
N. Heidfeld	Williams	29	Tyres
F. Massa	Sauber	28	Engine
M. Webber	Williams	20	Tyres

THE RACE

DRIVER	CAR	LAP	FASTEST LAP	TOP SPEED
J.P. Montoya	McLaren	39	1'24"770	330,3
K. Raikkonen	McLaren	40	1'25"030	329,2
F. Alonso	Renault	58	1'25"524	328,5
G. Fisichella	Renault	34	1'25"604	326,1
J. Button	BAR	58	1'25"790	320,6
T. Sato	BAR	54	1'25"858	324,4
J. Trulli	Toyota	52	1'26"178	329,0
C. Klien	Red Bull	58	1'26"374	323,8
D. Coulthard	Red Bull	58	1'26"417	326,9
F. Massa	Sauber	27	1'26"514	324,2
R. Barrichello	Ferrari	45	1'26"635	325,9
M. Webber	Williams	12	1'26"791	318,4
J. Villeneuve	Sauber	44	1'26"967	318,6
M. Schumacher	Ferrari	21	1'26"991	325,3
R. Schumacher	Toyota	38	1'27"025	323,1
N. Heidfeld	Williams	25	1'27"353	319,3
T. Monteiro	Jordan	50	1'29"035	323,2
R. Doornbos	Minardi	53	1'29"229	315,6
N. Karthikeyan	Jordan	42	1'29"286	324,5
C. Albers	Minardi	13	1'29"392	320,1

TURKISH GP

ISTANBUL
Length: **5,338 km**
Laps: **58**
Distance: **309,396 kms**

McLaren Misses Out on a 1-2 Finish

The new track designed by Hermann Tilke, who was also responsible
for Sepang and Shanghai, had an unusual baptism on Friday morning as the F1
drivers explored it on foot, by scooter (Schumacher) or by car. They were all intent
on familiarizing themselves with the secrets of the new circuit, which features
numerous ups and downs and wide run-off spaces.

Then the silence of the plateau on the outskirts of Istanbul was interrupted
by the roar of the engines and the drivers started to notch up the laps.
Numerous off-track excursions were made as they took their cars to the limit
and scrubbed off the dirt from the tarmac.

Not for the first time it was a reserve driver, in this case Zonta (Toyota),
who was quickest, but behind the Brazilian the McLarens were proving to be
in superb form once again.

Saturday confirmed this as Raikkonen set pole position, followed by Fisichella
while their respective team-mates, Montoya and Alonso, made up the second row.
At the lights Fisichella got a better start than Raikkonen, who was bottled
in by the two Renaults. But it didn't last long as the Finn powered into the lead
with a fantastic move, out-braking both Renaults and taking over at the front.
He went on to dominate the race and take the win.

Behind them the field started to break up and Massa, Ferrari's future driver,
made contact with Heidfeld and lost his front wing. It was a real shame as
the Brazilian had set an excellent eighth quickest time in qualifying.

The pit stops soon began and after 20 laps the two McLarens
found themselves in the lead by more than 20 seconds over Button and Alonso
while Fisichella was a bit behind because of yet another lengthy stop due
to problems with the refuelling rig.

At the race mid-point the positions were stable with the two McLarens
in the lead followed by the two Renaults, but Montoya made a risky passing
move on Monteiro two laps from the end, slammed on the brakes too early
and was hit by the Jordan driver, ruining his McLaren's suspension
and dropping down one place.

Alonso thus moved up to second place without any effort, depriving McLaren of a
certain 1-2. Fisichella was fourth, followed by Trulli, Button, Coulthard and Klien.
The weekend was one to forget for Ferrari, with Barrichello finishing tenth
and Schumacher retiring after making contact with Webber.

It was a very disappointing weekend also for Williams.
Both drivers had problems with their right rear tyres,
which suffered tyre failures in the early stages
of the Turkish GP. Mark Webber even suffered
the same fate twice.

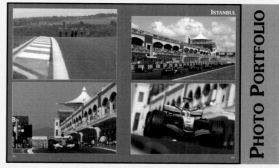

Another win for McLaren who put both
their drivers on the podium, while Alonso kept
a cool head to finish with a precious second place
on the brand-new circuit built on the outskirts
of Istanbul.

CHAMPIONSHIPS POINTS		AUSTRALIAN GP	MALAYSIAN GP	BAHRAIN GP	SAN MARINO GP	SPANISH GP	MONACO GP	EUROPEAN GP	CANADIAN GP	UNITED STATES GP	FRENCH GP	BRITISH GP	GERMAN GP	HUNGARIAN GP	TURKISH GP	ITALIAN GP	BELGIUM GP	BRAZILIAN GP	JAPANESE GP	CHINA GP	TOTAL POINT
1	F. ALONSO	6	10	10	10	8	5	10	-	rit.	10	8	10	-	8						95
2	K. RAIKKONEN	1	-	6	-	10	10	-	10	rit.	8	6	-	10	10						71
3	M. SCHUMACHER	-	2	-	8	-	2	4	8	10	6	3	4	8	-						55
4	J.P. MONTOYA	3	5	/	/	2	4	2	sq.	rit.	-	10	8	-	6						40
5	J. TRULLI	-	8	8	4	6	-	1	-	rit.	4	-	-	5	3						39
6	G. FISICHELLA	10	-	-	-	4	-	3	-	rit.	3	5	5	-	5						35
7	R. SCHUMACHER	-	4	5	-	5	3	-	3	rit.	2	1	3	6	-						32
8	R. BARRICHELLO	8	-	-	-	-	1	6	6	8	-	2	-	-	-						31
9	N. HEIDFELD	-	6	-	3	-	8	8	-	rit.	-	-	-	3	-						28
10	M. WEBBER	4	-	3	2	3	6	-	4	rit.	-	-	-	2	-						24
11	J. BUTTON	-	-	-	sq.	sq.	sq.	-	-	rit.	5	4	6	4	4						23
12	D. COULTHARD	5	3	1	-	1	-	5	2	rit.	-	-	2	-	2						21
13	F. MASSA	-	-	2	-	-	-	-	-	5	rit.	-	1	-	-						8
14	T. MONTEIRO	-	-	-	-	-	-	-	-	6	-	-	-	-	-						6
15	A. WURZ	/	/	/	6	/	/	/	/	/	/	/	/	/	/						6
16	J. VILLENEUVE	-	-	-	5	-	-	-	-	rit.	1	-	-	-	-						6
17	N. KARTHIKEYAN	-	-	-	-	-	-	-	-	5	-	-	-	-	-						5
18	C. KLIEN	2	1	-	/	-	-	-	1	rit.	-	-	-	-	1						5
19	C. ALBERS	-	-	-	-	-	-	-	-	4	-	-	-	-	-						4
20	P. DE LA ROSA	/	/	4	/	/	/	/	/	/	/	/	/	/	/						4
21	P. FRIESACHER	-	-	-	-	-	-	-	-	3	-	-	-	-	-						3
22	V. LIUZZI	/	/	/	1	/	/	/	/	/	/	/	/	/	/						1
23	T. SATO	-	-	-	sq.	sq.	sq.	-	-	rit.	-	-	-	1	-						1
24	A. DAVIDSON	-	-	-	/	/	/	/	/	/	/	/	/	-	-						0
25	R. DOORNBOS	/	/	/	/	/	/	/	/	/	/	/	/	-	-						0

rit.: Retired   **sq.**: Disqualified

POLE POSITION

'90	A. Senna	'98	M. Schumacher
'91	A. Senna	'99	M. Hakkinen
'92	N. Mansell	'00	M. Schumacher
'93	A. Prost	'01	J.P. Montoya
'94	J. Alesi	'02	J.P. Montoya
'95	D. Coulthard	'03	M. Schumacher
'96	D. Hill	'04	R. Barrichello
'97	J. Alesi	'05	J.P. Montoya

STARTING GRID

1
 JUAN PABLO MONTOYA — McLAREN
 FERNANDO ALONSO — RENAULT

2
 JENSON BUTTON — BAR
 TAKUMA SATO — BAR

3
 JARNO TRULLI — TOYOTA
 MICHAEL SCHUMACHER — FERRARI

4
 RUBENS BARRICHELLO — FERRARI
 GIANCARLO FISICHELLA — RENAULT

5
 RALF SCHUMACHER — TOYOTA
 DAVID COULTHARD — RED BULL

6
 KIMI RAIKKONEN — McLAREN
 JACQUES VILLENEUVE — SAUBER

7
 CHRISTIAN KLIEN — RED BULL
 MARK WEBBER — WILLIAMS

8
 FELIPE MASSA — SAUBER
 ANTONIO PIZZONIA — WILLIAMS

9
 TIAGO MONTEIRO — JORDAN
 ROBERT DOORNBOS — MINARDI

10
 NARAIN KARTHIKEYAN — JORDAN
 CHRISTIJAN ALBERS — MINARDI

	1°	2°	3°
'90	A. Senna	A. Prost	G. Berger
'91	N. Mansell	A. Senna	A. Prost
'92	A. Senna	M. Brundle	M. Schumacher
'93	D. Hill	J. Alesi	M. Andretti
'94	D. Hill	G. Berger	M. Hakkinen
'95	J. Herbert	M. Hakkinen	H.H. Frentzen
'96	M. Schumacher	J. Alesi	M. Hakkinen
'97	D. Coulthard	J. Alesi	H.H. Frentzen
'98	M. Schumacher	E. Irvine	R. Schumacher
'99	H.H. Frentzen	R. Schumacher	M. Salo
'00	M. Schumacher	M. Hakkinen	R. Schumacher
'01	J.P. Montoya	R. Barrichello	R. Schumacher
'02	R. Barrichello	M. Schumacher	E. Irvine
'03	M. Schumacher	J.P. Montoya	R. Barrichello
'04	R. Barrichello	M. Schumacher	J. Button

RESULTS

	DRIVER	CAR	KPH	GAP
1	J.P. Montoya	McLaren	247,096	-
2	F. Alonso	Renault	246,959	0'02"479
3	G. Fisichella	Renault	246,106	0'17"975
4	K. Raikkonen	McLaren	245,843	0'22"775
5	J. Trulli	Toyota	245,242	0'33"786
6	R. Schumacher	Toyota	244,691	0'43"925
7	A. Pizzonia	Williams	244,652	0'44"643
8	J. Button	BAR	243,627	1'03"635
9	F. Massa	Sauber	242,996	1'15"413
10	M. Schumacher	Ferrari	241,896	1'36"070
11	J. Villeneuve	Sauber	242,362	1 lap
12	R. Barrichello	Ferrari	242,163	1 lap
13	C. Klien	Red Bull	242,121	1 lap
14	M. Webber	Williams	242,052	1 lap
15	D. Coulthard	Red Bull	241,215	1 lap
16	T. Sato	BAR	241,164	1 lap
17	T. Monteiro	Jordan	237,041	2 laps
18	R. Doornbos	Minardi	236,437	2 laps
19	C. Albers	Minardi	234,713	2 laps
20	N. Karthikeyan	Jordan	229,136	3 laps

THE RACE

DRIVER	CAR	LAP	FASTEST LAP	TOP SPEED
K. Raikkonen	McLaren	51	1'21"504	370,1
J.P. Montoya	McLaren	15	1'21"828	366,1
F. Alonso	Renault	16	1'22"146	360,6
G. Fisichella	Renault	16	1'22"587	364,6
J. Trulli	Toyota	19	1'22"831	362,2
A. Pizzonia	Williams	21	1'22"870	364,4
M. Webber	Williams	40	1'22"935	365,8
R. Schumacher	Toyota	19	1'23"076	358,6
J. Button	BAR	16	1'23"161	359,1
T. Sato	BAR	14	1'23"341	364,1
F. Massa	Sauber	18	1'23"365	360,3
R. Barrichello	Ferrari	13	1'23"466	364,9
M. Schumacher	Ferrari	5	1'23"584	369,9
C. Klien	Red Bull	17	1'23"633	363,7
D. Coulthard	Red Bull	18	1'23"867	363,3
J. Villeneuve	Sauber	13	1'23"892	365,9
T. Monteiro	Jordan	9	1'24"810	360,8
C. Albers	Minardi	33	1'24"966	356,7
N. Karthikeyan	Jordan	17	1'25"146	357,6
R. Doornbos	Minardi	31	1'25"193	357,6

ITALIAN GP

MONTOYA KING OF MONZA

After the incredible record reached in pre-race practice when he broke through the 370 km/h barrier on the Monza straight, Juan Pablo had an almost perfect race weekend for McLaren, taking pole position and the win. Alongside the Colombian on the starting-grid was Alonso, the Spaniard in search of points to increase the gap to Raikkonen, while the Finn was eleventh on the grid due to an engine change after Saturday's session. Behind the front row were the two BARs, which as usual were extremely quick in qualifying.

The Italian GP, which is held on one of the fastest tracks in the world and where due to the usual problems with aerodynamics it becomes difficult to overtake, turned into a war of nerves.

Montoya was clear favourite, but the driver who had to make up the most places to get close to Alonso in the standings was Kimi Raikkonen. The Finn's secret aim however was to pass Fernando, get close to his team-mate and then take the lead either through his own ability or during the pit stops.

And the Finnish driver almost succeeded. After starting off with a strategy of attack based on one pit stop, he was in third place half-way through the race just before his scheduled visit.

Everything was going according to plan but three laps later Kimi had to come into the pits for an unplanned stop to change his rear tyre which was almost worn through.

At this point Alonso was virtually guaranteed his second place and despite the tyre problems that were also afflicting Montoya, he thought better not to force the pace that much. In addition Fisichella was right behind, ready to protect his team-mate from Raikkonen, who had slipped to fourth.

The GP concluded with Montoya winning his second race at Monza (his first was in 2001) and with the two Renault drivers accompanying him onto the podium. This result was a major step forward for the French manufacturer in its difficult quest for the Constructors' title, given the McLaren supremacy in the second half of the championship.

As mentioned before, Raikkonen came in fourth ahead of the two Toyotas of Trulli and Ralf Schumacher.

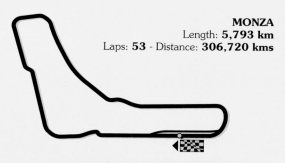

Antonio Pizzonia made his return to racing as a last-minute stand-in for Nick Heidfeld. The Brazilian drove an honest race to finish seventh, a result that brought a few smiles back to the Williams team, which was disenchanted with the poor performance of Mark Webber.

Fisichella finally stepped up onto the podium after a lengthy absence. The photo however is dedicated to Schumacher, a four-times winner at Monza, but only tenth at this finish this year, to the disappointment of the 100,000 tifosi present at the circuit.

	CHAMPIONSHIPS POINTS	AUSTRALIAN GP	MALAYSIAN GP	BAHRAIN GP	SAN MARINO GP	SPANISH GP	MONACO GP	EUROPEAN GP	CANADIAN GP	UNITED STATES GP	FRENCH GP	BRITISH GP	GERMAN GP	HUNGARIAN GP	TURKISH GP	ITALIAN GP	BELGIUM GP	BRAZILIAN GP	JAPANESE GP	CHINA GP	TOTAL POINT
1	F. ALONSO	6	10	10	10	8	5	10	-	rit.	10	8	10	-	8	8					103
2	K. RAIKKONEN	1	-	6	-	10	10	-	10	rit.	8	6	-	10	10	5					76
3	M. SCHUMACHER	-	2	-	8	-	2	4	8	10	6	3	4	8	-	-					55
4	J.P. MONTOYA	3	5	/	/	2	4	2	sq.	rit.	-	10	8	-	6	10					50
5	J. TRULLI	-	8	8	4	6	-	1	-	rit.	4	-	-	5	3	4					43
6	G. FISICHELLA	10	-	-	-	4	-	3	-	rit.	3	5	5	-	5	6					41
7	R. SCHUMACHER	-	4	5	-	5	3	-	3	rit.	2	1	3	6	-	3					35
8	R. BARRICHELLO	8	-	-	-	-	1	6	6	8	-	2	-	-	-	-					31
9	N. HEIDFELD	-	6	-	3	-	8	8	-	rit.	-	-	-	3	-	/					28
10	M. WEBBER	4	-	3	2	3	6	-	4	rit.	-	-	-	2	-	-					24
11	J. BUTTON	-	-	-	sq.	sq.	sq.	-	-	rit.	5	4	6	4	4	1					24
12	D. COULTHARD	5	3	1	-	1	-	5	2	rit.	-	-	2	-	2	-					21
13	F. MASSA	-	-	2	-	-	-	-	5	rit.	-	-	1	-	-	-					8
14	T. MONTEIRO	-	-	-	-	-	-	-	-	6	-	-	-	-	-	-					6
15	A. WURZ	/	/	/	6	/	/	/	/	/	/	/	/	/	/	/					6
16	J. VILLENEUVE	-	-	-	5	-	-	-	-	rit.	1	-	-	-	-	-					6
17	N. KARTHIKEYAN	-	-	-	-	-	-	-	-	5	-	-	-	-	-	-					5
18	C. KLIEN	2	1	-	/	/	/	-	1	rit.	-	-	-	-	1	-					5
19	C. ALBERS	-	-	-	-	-	-	-	-	4	-	-	-	-	-	-					4
20	P. DE LA ROSA	-	/	4	/	/	/	/	/	/	/	/	/	/	-	/					4
21	P. FRIESACHER	-	-	-	-	-	-	-	-	3	-	-	/	-	/	/					3
22	A. PIZZONIA	/	/	/	/	/	/	/	/	/	/	/	/	/	/	2					2
23	V. LIUZZI	/	/	/	1	-	-	-	-	/	-	-	/	/	-	/					1
24	T. SATO	-	-	-	sq.	sq.	sq.	-	-	rit.	-	-	-	1	-						1
25	A. DAVIDSON	/	-	/	-	/	/	/	/	/	/	/	/	/	-	/					0
26	R. DOORNBOS	/	/	/	/	/	/	/	/	/	/	/	/	-	-	-					0

rit.: Retired **sq.:** Disqualified

POLE POSITION

'90	A. Senna	'98	M. Hakkinen
'91	A. Senna	'99	M. Hakkinen
'92	N. Mansell	'00	M. Hakkinen
'93	A. Prost	'01	J.P. Montoya
'94	R. Barrichello	'02	M. Schumacher
'95	G. Berger	'03	-
'96	J. Villeneuve	'04	J. Trulli
'97	J. Villeneuve	'05	J.P. Montoya

STARTING GRID

1
 JUAN PABLO MONTOYA McLAREN
 KIMI RAIKKONEN McLAREN

2
 JARNO TRULLI TOYOTA
 FERNANDO ALONSO RENAULT

3
 RALF SCHUMACHER TOYOTA
 MICHAEL SCHUMACHER FERRARI

4
 FELIPE MASSA SAUBER
 JENSON BUTTON BAR

5
 MARK WEBBER WILLIAMS
 TAKUMA SATO BAR

6
 DAVID COULTHARD RED BULL
 RUBENS BARRICHELLO FERRARI

7
 GIANCARLO FISICHELLA RENAULT
 JACQUES VILLENEUVE SAUBER

8
 ANTONIO PIZZONIA WILLIAMS
 CHRISTIAN KLIEN RED BULL

9
 ROBERT DOORNBOS MINARDI
 CHRISTIJAN ALBERS MINARDI

10
 TIAGO MONTEIRO JORDAN
 NARAIN KARTHIKEYAN JORDAN

	1°	2°	3°
'90	A. Senna	A. Prost	G. Berger
'91	A. Senna	G. Berger	N. Piquet
'92	M. Schumacher	N. Mansell	R. Patrese
'93	D. Hill	M. Schumacher	A. Prost
'94	D. Hill	M. Hakkinen	J. Verstappen
'95	M. Schumacher	D. Hill	M. Brundle
'96	M. Schumacher	J. Villeneuve	M. Hakkinen
'97	M. Schumacher	G. Fisichella	M. Hakkinen
'98	D. Hill	R. Schumacher	J. Alesi
'99	D. Coulthard	M. Hakkinen	H.H. Frentzen
'00	M. Hakkinen	M. Schumacher	R. Schumacher
'01	M. Schumacher	D. Coulthard	G. Fisichella
'02	M. Schumacher	R. Barrichello	J.P. Montoya
'03	-	-	-
'04	K. Raikkonen	M. Schumacher	R. Barrichello

RESULTS

	DRIVER	CAR	KPH	GAP
1	K. Raikkonen	McLaren	204,568	-
2	F. Alonso	Renault	203,499	0'28"394
3	J. Button	BAR	203,361	0'32"077
4	M. Webber	Williams	201,982	1'09"167
5	R. Barrichello	Ferrari	201,651	1'18"136
6	J. Villeneuve	Sauber	201,310	1'27"435
7	R. Schumacher	Toyota	201,305	1'27"574
8	T. Monteiro	Jordan	199,893	1 lap
9	C. Klien	Red Bull	199,402	1 lap
10	F. Massa	Sauber	198,036	1 lap
11	N. Karthikeyan	Jordan	197,988	1 lap
12	C. Albers	Minardi	191,904	2 laps
13	R. Doornbos	Minardi	189,729	3 laps

RETIREMENTS

J.P. Montoya	McLaren	40	Accident
A. Pizzonia	Williams	40	Accident
J. Trulli	Toyota	34	Crashed
D. Coulthard	Red Bull	18	Engine
M. Schumacher	Ferrari	13	Accident
T. Sato	BAR	13	Accident
G. Fisichella	Renault	10	Crashed

THE RACE

DRIVER	CAR	LAP	FASTEST LAP	TOP SPEED
R. Schumacher	Toyota	43	1'51"453	304,9
M. Webber	Williams	44	1'52"287	308,5
C. Klien	Red Bull	43	1'52"582	311,0
R. Barrichello	Ferrari	44	1'52"590	308,1
J. Button	BAR	44	1'53"323	306,8
K. Raikkonen	McLaren	34	1'53"810	313,1
J. Villeneuve	Sauber	44	1'54"251	314,1
N. Karthikeyan	Jordan	43	1'55"885	305,0
J.P. Montoya	McLaren	14	1'55"988	313,4
F. Alonso	Renault	31	1'56"131	316,4
J. Trulli	Toyota	3	1'56"953	307,1
G. Fisichella	Renault	9	1'57"117	317,7
M. Schumacher	Ferrari	10	1'57"444	309,0
T. Sato	BAR	10	1'57"534	308,8
A. Pizzonia	Williams	32	1'57"541	310,1
F. Massa	Sauber	28	1'57"748	312,5
T. Monteiro	Jordan	41	1'57"886	302,2
D. Coulthard	Red Bull	8	1'58"451	310,3
R. Doornbos	Minardi	38	2'01"148	310,9
C. Albers	Minardi	6	2'01"627	310,3

BELGIAN GP

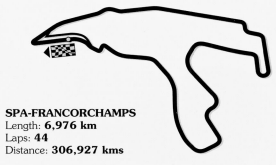

SPA-FRANCORCHAMPS
Length: **6,976 km**
Laps: **44**
Distance: **306,927 kms**

MCLAREN'S ILLUSIONS DASHED

Ron Dennis was walking around in a happy mood on Saturday at the end of qualifying, after his two McLaren drivers had taken the top two grid slots, something that had last occurred at Imola in 2001.

Montoya first and Raikkonen second, finally without any engine problems. Behind them was a fantastic Jarno Trulli (Toyota) and Fernando Alonso (Renault), followed by the Schumacher brothers.

This time Fisichella was the unlucky one, the Italian dropping down ten places on the grid to row 7 because of an engine change. At a circuit like Spa this was a tough position to start from due to the first dog-leg curve immediately after the start which always produced a traffic jam and often a pile-up, while the threat of rain was also bound to shake things up as well.

This time the start passed by without a hitch and Montoya powered away with his team-mate behind, followed by Trulli and Alonso, who went wide at the first corner to avoid any risk of contact.

Montoya dominantly led the field on a still damp track due to the rain that had fallen shortly before the race, and the Colombian was shadowed by Raikkonen. On lap 10 the safety car came out after Giancarlo Fisichella crashed at Eau Rouge, the Italian losing control of his Renault and slamming into the guardrail. Everything appeared to be going according to plan: Montoya's pit stop was a bit long and Raikkonen moved into the lead without too much fuss.

If things stayed that way, Kimi would cut the gap to Alonso and McLaren would pick up the maximum 18 points for the Constructors' battle.

But the party was ruined by Pizzonia, who came out of the pits, slid sideways while Montoya was arriving and sent him into the wall. It was an incredible move but one that had happened before due to the tight curve coming out of the pit lane, right at the point where the cars accelerate.

Raikkonen went on to win but Alonso was runner-up and the Finn only picked up two points in the standings. Third place went to Button, who drive a great race from the back, overtaking several drivers after dropping down to thirteenth due to a wrong choice of tyre.

The legendary Spa-Francorchamps circuit once again produced a race full of surprises, in particular due to the adverse weather conditions.
Showers and a damp track created all sorts of difficulty in the choice of tyres. Montoya paid the consequences to the full after Pizzonia slid into him coming out of the pit lane, but Trulli, Schumacher and Barrichello also came off badly.

After the quickest circuit on the calendar, the championship moved to the most beautiful and most challenging, with its numerous elevation changes, surrounding forests and constantly changing weather conditions.

CHAMPIONSHIPS POINTS		AUSTRALIAN GP	MALAYSIAN GP	BAHRAIN GP	SAN MARINO GP	SPANISH GP	MONACO GP	EUROPEAN GP	CANADIAN GP	UNITED STATES GP	FRENCH GP	BRITISH GP	GERMAN GP	HUNGARIAN GP	TURKISH GP	ITALIAN GP	BELGIUM GP	BRAZILIAN GP	JAPANESE GP	CHINA GP	TOTAL POINT
1	F. ALONSO	6	10	10	10	8	5	10	-	rit.	10	8	10	-	8	8	8				111
2	K. RAIKKONEN	1	-	6	-	10	10	-	10	rit.	8	6	-	10	10	5	10				86
3	M. SCHUMACHER	-	2	-	8	-	2	4	8	10	6	3	4	8	-	-	-				55
4	J.P. MONTOYA	3	5	/	/	2	4	2	sq.	rit.	-	10	8	-	6	10	-				50
5	J. TRULLI	-	8	8	4	6	-	1	-	rit.	4	-	-	5	3	4	-				43
6	G. FISICHELLA	10	-	-	-	4	-	3	-	rit.	3	5	5	-	5	6	-				41
7	R. SCHUMACHER	-	4	5	-	5	3	-	3	rit.	2	1	3	6	-	3	2				37
8	R. BARRICHELLO	8	-	-	-	-	1	6	6	8	-	2	-	-	-	-	4				35
9	J. BUTTON	-	-	-	sq.	sq.	sq.	-	-	rit.	5	4	6	4	4	1	6				30
10	M. WEBBER	4	-	3	2	3	6	-	4	rit.	-	-	-	2	-	-	5				29
11	N. HEIDFELD	-	6	-	3	-	8	8	-	rit.	-	-	-	3	-	/	/				28
12	D. COULTHARD	5	3	1	-	1	-	5	2	rit.	-	-	2	-	2	-	-				21
13	J. VILLENEUVE	-	-	-	5	-	-	-	-	rit.	1	-	-	-	-	-	3				9
14	F. MASSA	-	-	2	-	-	-	-	5	rit.	-	-	1	-	-	-	-				8
15	T. MONTEIRO	-	-	-	-	-	-	-	-	6	-	-	-	-	-	-	1				7
16	A. WURZ	/	/	/	6	/	/	/	/	/	/	/	/	/	/	-	-				6
17	N. KARTHIKEYAN	-	-	-	-	-	-	-	-	5	-	-	-	-	-	-	-				5
18	C. KLIEN	2	1	-	/	/	/	/	1	rit.	-	-	-	-	1	-	-				5
19	C. ALBERS	-	-	-	-	-	-	-	-	4	-	-	-	-	-	-	-				4
20	P. DE LA ROSA	/	/	4	/	/	/	/	/	/	-	/	/	/	/	-	/				4
21	P. FRIESACHER	-	-	-	-	-	-	-	-	3	-	-	-	/	/	/	/				3
22	A. PIZZONIA	/	/	/	/	/	/	/	/	/	/	/	/	/	/	2	-				2
23	V. LIUZZI	/	/	/	1	-	-	-	-	/	/	/	/	/	/	/	/				1
24	T. SATO	-	-	-	sq.	sq.	sq.	-	-	rit.	-	-	-	1	-	-	-				1
25	A. DAVIDSON	/	-	/	/	/	/	/	/	/	/	/	/	/	-	-	-				0
26	R. DOORNBOS	/	/	/	/	/	/	/	/	/	/	/	-	-	-	-	-				0

rit.: Retired   **sq.**: Disqualified

POLE POSITION

'90	A. Senna	'98	M. Hakkinen
'91	A. Senna	'99	M. Hakkinen
'92	N. Mansell	'00	M. Hakkinen
'93	A. Prost	'01	M. Schumacher
'94	A. Senna	'02	J.P. Montoya
'95	D. Hill	'03	R. Barrichello
'96	D. Hill	'04	R. Barrichello
'97	J. Villeneuve	'05	F. Alonso

STARTING GRID

 FERNANDO ALONSO RENAULT — 1 — **JUAN PABLO MONTOYA** MCLAREN

 GIANCARLO FISICHELLA RENAULT — 2 — **JENSON BUTTON** BAR

 KIMI RAIKKONEN MCLAREN — 3 — **CHRISTIAN KLIEN** RED BULL

 MICHAEL SCHUMACHER FERRARI — 4 — **FELIPE MASSA** SAUBER

 RUBENS BARRICHELLO FERRARI — 5 — **RALF SCHUMACHER** TOYOTA

 JACQUES VILLENEUVE SAUBER — 6 — **TIAGO MONTEIRO** JORDAN

 MARK WEBBER WILLIAMS — 7 — **ANTONIO PIZZONIA** WILLIAMS

 DAVID COULTHARD RED BULL — 8 — **NARAIN KARTHIKEYAN** JORDAN

 CHRISTIJAN ALBERS MINARDI — 9 — **JARNO TRULLI** TOYOTA

 ROBERT DOORNBOS MINARDI — 10 — **TAKUMA SATO** BAR

	1°	2°	3°
'90	A. Prost	G. Berger	A. Senna
'91	A. Senna	R. Patrese	G. Berger
'92	N. Mansell	R. Patrese	M. Schumacher
'93	A. Senna	D. Hill	M. Schumacher
'94	M. Schumacher	D. Hill	J. Alesi
'95	G. Berger	M. Hakkinen	J. Alesi
'96	D. Hill	J. Alesi	M. Schumacher
'97	J. Villeneuve	G. Berger	O. Panis
'98	M. Hakkinen	D. Coulthard	M. Schumacher
'99	M. Hakkinen	M. Schumacher	H.H. Frentzen
'00	M. Schumacher	G. Fisichella	H.H. Frentzen
'01	D. Coulthard	M. Schumacher	N. Heidfeld
'02	M. Schumacher	R. Schumacher	D. Coulthard
'03	K. Raikkonen	G. Fisichella	F. Alonso
'04	J.P. Montoya	K. Raikkonen	R. Barrichello

RESULTS

	DRIVER	CAR	KPH	GAP
1	J.P. Montoya	McLaren	205,439	-
2	K. Raikkonen	McLaren	205,342	0'02"527
3	F. Alonso	Renault	204,491	0'24"840
4	M. Schumacher	Ferrari	204,081	0'35"668
5	G. Fisichella	Renault	203,909	0'40"218
6	R. Barrichello	Ferrari	202,822	1'09"173
7	J. Button	BAR	202,404	1 lap
8	R. Schumacher	Toyota	202,365	1 lap
9	C. Klien	Red Bull	202,239	1 lap
10	T. Sato	BAR	200,861	1 lap
11	F. Massa	Sauber	200,449	1 lap
12	J. Villeneuve	Sauber	200,419	1 lap
13	J. Trulli	Toyota	200,243	2 laps
14	C. Albers	Minardi	197,237	2 laps
15	N. Karthikeyan	Jordan	196,393	3 laps

RETIREMENTS

T. Monteiro	Jordan	55	Engine
M. Webber	Williams	45	Not qualified
R. Doornbos	Minardi	34	Engine
D. Coulthard	Red Bull	0	Accident
A. Pizzonia	Williams	0	Accident

THE RACE

DRIVER	CAR	LAP	FASTEST LAP	TOP SPEED
K. Raikkonen	McLaren	29	1'12"268	326,8
J.P. Montoya	McLaren	27	1'12"650	324,7
F. Alonso	Renault	21	1'12"653	323,4
M. Schumacher	Ferrari	25	1'12"800	322,5
G. Fisichella	Renault	11	1'13"190	324,7
R. Barrichello	Ferrari	49	1'13"192	319,3
J. Trulli	Toyota	69	1'13"570	318,3
M. Webber	Williams	45	1'13"590	318,5
R. Schumacher	Toyota	25	1'13"724	318,5
J. Button	BAR	24	1'13"746	319,0
C. Klien	Red Bull	50	1'13"800	319,4
J. Villeneuve	Sauber	25	1'14"054	316,3
F. Massa	Sauber	70	1'14"343	324,2
T. Sato	BAR	32	1'14"394	318,0
N. Karthikeyan	Jordan	41	1'14"906	316,9
T. Monteiro	Jordan	41	1'15"113	314,3
C. Albers	Minardi	19	1'15"527	315,2
R. Doornbos	Minardi	16	1'15"792	306,0
D. Coulthard	Red Bull	-		
A. Pizzonia	Williams	-		

BRAZILIAN GP

INTERLAGOS
Length: **4,309 km**
Laps: **71** - Distance: **305,909 kms**

ALONSO - WORLD CHAMPION!

The 2005 championship was destined to finish in one way, and it happened
in Brazil, when Fernando Alonso became the youngest-ever world Formula 1
champion at just over 24 years of age. The Spaniard followed on from
the great Michael Schumacher, who won the world title seven times,
including five on the run from 2000 to 2004.
The Spanish youngster won the title at the tricky Interlagos circuit.
He set pole position and then throughout the race played it safe in third place,
a position that would mathematically guarantee him the title.
The win went to McLsren, with Montoya taking the chequered flag ahead
of Raikkonen, but the Drivers' title went to Alonso thanks to the points lead
he had accumulated in the first part of the season, while the McLarens
were losing pieces and points at each race.
Had they not had such a poor start to the season things would surely
have been different, judging by the superiority shown by the Silver Arrows
in the last few races.
It should be pointed out however that a champion also becomes
a champion by the way he manages the situation in difficult moments,
and Alonso was able to do this with consummate ease.
In the Brazilian race he held the lead for two laps, then Montoya passed him
with apparent ease, and he slipped down to third when Raikkonen did the same.
The two McLarens swapped the lead of the race while all Alonso
had to do was keep the Ferrari of Schummy behind him, because he knew
that a third place would automatically mean that he was champion.
That was the way they finished, with Fisichella in fifth place followed
by Barrichello, Button and Ralf Schumacher.
What about the Williams? This time it wasn't the fault of the drivers
that there was no trace of the British cars in the final results.
Shortly after the start in fact David Coulthard tried to dive into a gap that was not
there and took out both BMW-Williams, destroying his Red Bull and Pizzonia's
car, while Webber limped back to the pits for major repairs. The Australian
would later return to the race 26 laps behind and was not classified.

Fernando Alonso made his Formula 1 debut
at 19 years of age in the 2001 Australian GP.
He set his first pole position in Malaysia in 2003
and on that same weekend stepped up onto the podium
for the very first time. His first grand prix win came
in Hungary later that year. He became World Champion
with two rounds left to run in the 2005 season.

Alonso became this year's world champion with
third place at Interlagos behind the two McLarens.
Celebrations in the Renault garage, while over
at Williams they were assessing the damage
from two cars destroyed in the accident caused
by David Coulthard.

	CHAMPIONSHIPS POINTS	AUSTRALIAN GP	MALAYSIAN GP	BAHRAIN GP	SAN MARINO GP	SPANISH GP	MONACO GP	EUROPEAN GP	CANADIAN GP	UNITED STATES GP	FRENCH GP	BRITISH GP	GERMAN GP	HUNGARIAN GP	TURKISH GP	ITALIAN GP	BELGIUM GP	BRAZILIAN GP	JAPANESE GP	CHINA GP	TOTAL POINT
1	F. ALONSO	6	10	10	10	8	5	10	-	rit.	10	8	10	-	8	8	8	6			117
2	K. RAIKKONEN	1	-	6	-	10	10	-	10	rit.	8	6	-	10	10	5	10	8			94
3	M. SCHUMACHER	-	2	-	8	-	2	4	8	10	6	3	4	8	-	-	-	5			60
4	J.P. MONTOYA	3	5	/	/	2	4	2	sq.	rit.	-	10	8	-	6	10	-	10			60
5	G. FISICHELLA	10	-	-	-	4	-	3	-	rit.	3	5	5	-	5	6	-	4			45
6	J. TRULLI	-	8	8	4	6	-	1	-	rit.	4	-	-	5	3	4	-	-			43
7	R. SCHUMACHER	-	4	5	-	5	3	-	3	rit.	2	1	3	6	-	3	2	1			38
8	R. BARRICHELLO	8	-	-	-	-	1	6	6	8	-	2	-	-	-	-	4	3			38
9	J. BUTTON	-	-	-	sq.	sq.	sq.	-	-	rit.	5	4	6	4	4	1	6	2			32
10	M. WEBBER	4	-	3	2	3	6	-	4	rit.	-	-	-	2	-	-	5	-			29
11	N. HEIDFELD	-	6	-	3	-	8	8	-	rit.	-	-	-	3	-	/	/	/			28
12	D. COULTHARD	5	3	1	-	1	-	5	2	rit.	-	-	2	-	2	-	-	-			21
13	J. VILLENEUVE	-	-	-	5	-	-	-	-	rit.	1	-	-	-	-	-	3	-			9
14	F. MASSA	-	-	2	-	-	-	-	5	rit.	-	-	1	-	-	-	-	-			8
15	T. MONTEIRO	-	-	-	-	-	-	-	-	6	-	-	-	-	-	-	-	1			7
16	A. WURZ	/	/	/	6	/	/	/	/	/	/	/	/	/	/	/	/	/			6
17	N. KARTHIKEYAN	-	-	-	-	-	-	-	-	5	-	-	-	-	-	-	-	-			5
18	C. KLIEN	2	1	-	-	-	-	-	1	rit.	-	-	-	-	1	-	-	-			5
19	C. ALBERS	-	-	-	-	-	-	-	-	4	-	-	-	-	-	-	-	-			4
20	P. DE LA ROSA	/	/	4	/	/	/	/	/	/	/	/	/	/	/	/	/	/			4
21	P. FRIESACHER	-	-	-	-	-	-	-	-	3	-	-	-	-	-	-	-	-			3
22	A. PIZZONIA	/	/	/	/	/	/	/	/	/	/	/	/	/	/	/	2	/			2
23	V. LIUZZI	/	/	/	1	/	/	-	-	-	-	-	-	-	-	-	-	-			1
24	T. SATO	-	-	-	sq.	sq.	sq.	-	-	rit.	-	-	-	-	1	-	-	-			1
25	A. DAVIDSON	-	-	-	-	-	-	-	-	-	-	-	-	-	-	-	-	-			0
26	R. DOORNBOS	/	/	/	/	/	/	/	/	/	/	/	/	/	/	/	/	/			0

rit.: Retired   **sq.**: Disqualified

POLE POSITION

'90	A. Senna	'98	M. Schumacher
'91	G. Berger	'99	M. Schumacher
'92	N. Mansell	'00	M. Schumacher
'93	A. Prost	'01	M. Schumacher
'94	M. Schumacher	'02	M. Schumacher
'95	M. Schumacher	'03	R. Barrichello
'96	J. Villeneuve	'04	M. Schumacher
'97	J. Villeneuve	'05	R. Schumacher

STARTING GRID

1
 RALF SCHUMACHER TOYOTA
 JENSON BUTTON BAR

2
 GIANCARLO FISICHELLA RENAULT
 CHRISTIAN KLIEN RED BULL

3
 TAKUMA SATO BAR
 DAVID COULTHARD RED BULL

4
 MARK WEBBER WILLIAMS
 JACQUES VILLENEUVE SAUBER

5
 RUBENS BARRICHELLO FERRARI
 FELIPE MASSA SAUBER

6
 NARAIN KARTHIKEYAN JORDAN
 ANTONIO PIZZONIA WILLIAMS

7
 CHRISTIJAN ALBERS MINARDI
 MICHAEL SCHUMACHER FERRARI

8
 ROBERT DOORNBOS MINARDI
 FERNANDO ALONSO RENAULT

9
 KIMI RAIKKONEN McLAREN
 JUAN PABLO MONTOYA McLAREN

10
 JARNO TRULLI TOYOTA
 TIAGO MONTEIRO JORDAN

	1°	2°	3°
'90	N. Piquet	R. Moreno	A. Suzuki
'91	G. Berger	A. Senna	R. Patrese
'92	R. Patrese	G. Berger	M. Brundle
'93	A. Senna	A. Prost	M. Hakkinen
'94	D. Hill	M. Schumacher	J. Alesi
'95	M. Schumacher	M. Hakkinen	J. Herbert
'96	D. Hill	M. Schumacher	M. Hakkinen
'97	M. Schumacher	H.H. Frentzen	E. Irvine
'98	M. Hakkinen	E. Irvine	D. Coulthard
'99	M. Hakkinen	M. Schumacher	E. Irvine
'00	M. Schumacher	M. Hakkinen	D. Coulthard
'01	M. Schumacher	J.P. Montoya	D. Coulthard
'02	M. Schumacher	R. Barrichello	K. Raikkonen
'03	R. Barrichello	K. Raikkonen	D. Coulthard
'04	M. Schumacher	R. Schumacher	J. Button

RESULTS

	DRIVER	CAR	KPH	GAP
1	K. Raikkonen	McLaren	207,266	-
2	G. Fisichella	Renault	207,203	0'01"633
3	F. Alonso	Renault	206,591	0'17"456
4	M. Webber	Williams	206,406	0'22"274
5	J. Button	BAR	206,128	0'29"507
6	D. Coulthard	Red Bull	206,047	0'31"601
7	M. Schumacher	Ferrari	205,960	0'33"879
8	R. Schumacher	Toyota	205,362	0'49"548
9	C. Klien	Red Bull	205,271	0'51"925
10	F. Massa	Sauber	205,059	0'57"509
11	R. Barrichello	Ferrari	204,940	1'00"633
12	J. Villeneuve	Sauber	204,087	1'23"221
13	T. Monteiro	Jordan	199,633	1 lap
14	R. Doornbos	Minardi	199,009	2 laps
15	N. Karthikeyan	Jordan	197,599	2 laps
16	C. Albers	Minardi	190,985	4 laps

RETIREMENTS

A. Pizzonia	Williams	9	Spin
J. Trulli	Toyota	9	Accident
J.P. Montoya	McLaren	0	Crashed
T. Sato	BAR	52	Disqualified

THE RACE

DRIVER	CAR	LAP	FASTEST LAP	TOP SPEED
K. Raikkonen	McLaren	44	1'31"540	322,1
F. Alonso	Renault	21	1'31"599	323,0
G. Fisichella	Renault	19	1'32"522	318,3
J. Button	BAR	19	1'32"754	311,6
M. Schumacher	Ferrari	25	1'32"763	316,9
R. Schumacher	Toyota	9	1'32"795	313,0
M. Webber	Williams	21	1'33"022	315,3
D. Coulthard	Red Bull	18	1'33"023	309,2
R. Barrichello	Ferrari	52	1'33"133	317,4
F. Massa	Sauber	43	1'33"232	313,4
J. Villeneuve	Sauber	50	1'33"288	313,4
C. Klien	Red Bull	49	1'33"499	301,3
T. Sato	BAR	28	1'34"186	310,1
T. Monteiro	Jordan	17	1'35"458	295,6
N. Karthikeyan	Jordan	11	1'35"887	301,3
C. Albers	Minardi	33	1'36"039	299,0
R. Doornbos	Minardi	50	1'36"574	298,3
A. Pizzonia	Williams	9	1'36"711	302,4
J. Trulli	Toyota	9	1'37"428	289,0
J.P. Montoya	McLaren	-	-	-

JAPANESE GP

SUZUKA
Length: **5,807 km**
Laps: **53**
Distance: **307,573 kms**

KIMI'S SEVENTH SAMURAI!

The rain on Saturday, which got worse half-way through the session, threw a spanner into the normal starting-grid qualifying procedure and allowed Christian Klien (Red Bull) to take the fourth quickest time. Karthikeyan (Jordan) was eleventh and Albers (Minardi) thirteenth, while Schumacher, Alonso, Raikkonen, Montoya and Trulli were all relegated down the grid.

The race promised to be an interesting one and full of overtaking due to the unusual grid line-up and so it proved. Ralf Schumacher got a good start and held the lead of the race for twelve laps before coming into the pits for his first refuelling stop.

Behind the spectacle was an incredible one. Raikkonen passed five cars on the opening lap and continued in the same vein to move into second position by the mid-point of the race.

But Alonso was no less incisive and the new world champion pulled out a series of superb passing moves, including one on Schumacher. He even overtook Klien by cutting the chicane, decided to let him back through and then passed him for the second time.

Meanwhile Fisichella, who had started third on the grid, took over the lead of the race. It seemed that the Renault driver was heading for an easy win, even though a fast-recovering Raikkonen (McLaren) was getting closer and closer. A few laps from the end however Fisichella's Renault was clearly in difficulty and the gap to Raikkonen was getting visibly smaller. The Finn eventually passed him on the final lap to take the win.

It was appalling luck for the Italian but he would most probably have had problems anyway holding off such a competitive McLaren.

Alonso took the final podium slot followed by Webber, who finally put together a good race, Button, Coulthard and the two Schumacher brothers.

Since the start of the year, when he was a friendly newcomer to the Formula 1 scene, Takuma Sato has rapidly been turning into the terror of his fellow drivers. A series of reckless manoeuvres have created problems for several drivers, including Michael Schumacher in the Brazilian GP, when the German gave him a smack around his helmet after being punted off the track, as well as Jarno Trulli in Japan, who was forced to retire after coming into violent contact with Sato during the ninth lap.

At the Honda-owned circuit in the middle of a funfair park, two 'Japanese' cars took the front row of the grid, Ralf Schumacher in the Toyota and Jenson Button in the BAR. But at the flag the winner was once again Raikkonen.

	CHAMPIONSHIPS POINTS	AUSTRALIAN GP	MALAYSIAN GP	BAHRAIN GP	SAN MARINO GP	SPANISH GP	MONACO GP	EUROPEAN GP	CANADIAN GP	UNITED STATES GP	FRENCH GP	BRITISH GP	GERMAN GP	HUNGARIAN GP	TURKISH GP	ITALIAN GP	BELGIUM GP	BRAZILIAN GP	JAPANESE GP	CHINA GP	TOTAL POINT
1	F. ALONSO	6	10	10	10	8	5	10	-	rit.	10	8	10	-	8	8	8	6	6		123
2	K. RAIKKONEN	1	-	6	-	10	10	-	10	rit.	8	6	-	10	10	5	10	8	10		104
3	M. SCHUMACHER	-	2	-	8	-	2	4	8	10	6	3	4	8	-	-	-	5	2		62
4	J.P. MONTOYA	3	5	/	/	2	4	2	sq.	rit.	-	10	8	-	6	10	-	10	-		60
5	G. FISICHELLA	10	-	-	-	4	-	3	-	rit.	3	5	5	-	5	6	-	4	8		53
6	J. TRULLI	-	8	8	4	6	-	1	-	rit.	4	-	-	5	3	4	-	-	-		43
7	R. SCHUMACHER	-	4	5	-	5	3	-	3	rit.	2	1	3	6	-	3	2	1	1		39
8	R. BARRICHELLO	8	-	-	-	-	1	6	6	8	-	2	-	-	-	-	4	3	-		38
9	J. BUTTON	-	-	-	sq.	sq.	sq.	-	-	rit.	5	4	6	4	4	1	6	2	4		36
10	M. WEBBER	4	-	3	2	3	6	-	4	rit.	-	-	-	2	-	-	5	-	5		34
11	N. HEIDFELD	-	6	-	3	-	8	8	-	rit.	-	-	-	3	-	/	/	/	/		28
12	D. COULTHARD	5	3	1	-	1	-	5	2	rit.	-	-	2	-	2	-	-	-	3		24
13	J. VILLENEUVE	-	-	-	5	-	-	-	-	rit.	1	-	-	-	-	-	3	-	-		9
14	F. MASSA	-	-	2	-	-	-	-	5	rit.	-	-	1	-	-	-	-	-	-		8
15	T. MONTEIRO	-	-	-	-	-	-	-	6	-	-	-	-	-	-	-	1	-	-		7
16	A. WURZ	/	/	/	6	/	/	/	/	/	/	-	-	-	-	-	-	-	-		6
17	N. KARTHIKEYAN	-	-	-	-	-	-	-	5	-	-	-	-	-	-	-	-	-	-		5
18	C. KLIEN	2	1	-	-	-	-	-	1	rit.	-	-	-	1	-	-	-	-	-		5
19	C. ALBERS	-	-	-	-	-	-	-	4	-	-	-	-	-	-	-	-	-	-		4
20	P. DE LA ROSA	/	/	4	/	/	/	/	/	/	/	-	-	-	-	-	-	-	-		4
21	P. FRIESACHER	-	-	-	-	-	-	-	3	-	-	-	-	-	-	-	-	-	-		3
22	A. PIZZONIA	/	/	/	/	/	/	/	/	/	/	-	-	-	2	-	-	-	-		2
23	V. LIUZZI	/	/	/	1	-	-	-	-	/	/	-	-	-	-	-	-	-	-		1
24	T. SATO	-	-	-	sq.	sq.	sq.	-	-	rit.	-	-	-	1	-	-	-	-	-		1
25	A. DAVIDSON	-	-	/	/	/	/	/	/	/	/	-	-	-	-	-	-	-	-		0
26	R. DOORNBOS	/	/	/	/	/	/	/	/	/	-	-	/	-	-	-	-	-	-		0

rit.: Retired   **sq.**: Disqualified

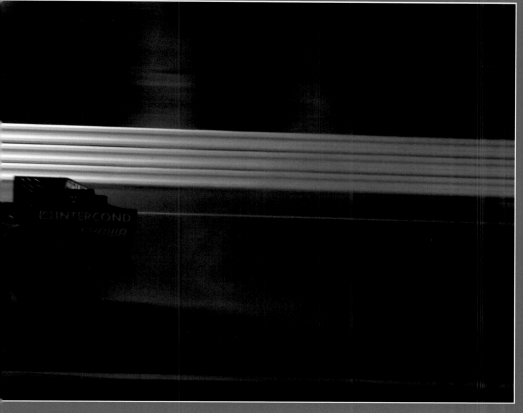

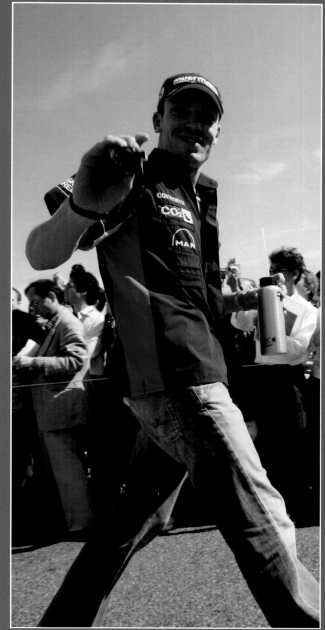

POLE POSITION

'04 R. Barrichello
'05 F. Alonso

1°	2°	3°
'04 R. Barrichello	J. Button	K. Raikkonen

STARTING GRID

1
 FERNANDO ALONSO — RENAULT
 GIANCARLO FISICHELLA — RENAULT

2
 KIMI RAIKKONEN — MCLAREN
 JENSON BUTTON — BAR

3
 JUAN PABLO MONTOYA — MCLAREN
 MICHAEL SCHUMACHER — FERRARI

4
 DAVID COULTHARD — RED BULL
 RUBENS BARRICHELLO — FERRARI

5
 RALF SCHUMACHER — TOYOTA
 MARK WEBBER — WILLIAMS

6
 FELIPE MASSA — SAUBER
 JARNO TRULLI — TOYOTA

7
 ANTONIO PIZZONIA — WILLIAMS
 CHRISTIAN KLIEN — RED BULL

8
 NARAIN KARTHIKEYAN — JORDAN
 JACQUES VILLENEUVE — SAUBER

9
 TAKUMA SATO — BAR
 CHRISTIJAN ALBERS — MINARDI

10
 TIAGO MONTEIRO — JORDAN
 ROBERT DOORNBOS — MINARDI

RESULTS

	DRIVER	CAR	KPH	GAP
1	F. Alonso	Renault	183,234	-
2	K. Raikkonen	McLaren	183,111	0'04"015
3	R. Schumacher	Toyota	182,461	0'25"376
4	G. Fisichella	Renault	182,439	0'26"114
5	C. Klien	Red Bull	182,266	0'31"839
6	F. Massa	Sauber	182,128	0'36"400
7	M. Webber	Williams	182,115	0'36"842
8	J. Button	BAR	181,982	0'41"249
9	D. Coulthard	Red Bull	181,891	0'44"247
10	J. Villeneuve	Sauber	181,419	0'59"977
11	T. Monteiro	Jordan	180,682	1'24"648
12	R. Barrichello	Ferrari	180,440	1'32"812
13	A. Pizzonia	Williams	180,858	1 lap
14	R. Doornbos	Minardi	179,970	1 lap
15	J. Trulli	Toyota	178,093	1 lap
16	C. Albers	Minardi	174,331	5 laps

RETIREMENTS

T. Sato	BAR	34	Gearbox
N. Karthikeyan	Jordan	28	Crashed
J.P. Montoya	McLaren	24	Suspension
M. Schumacher	Ferrari	22	Spin

THE RACE

DRIVER	CAR	LAP	FASTEST LAP	TOP SPEED
K. Raikkonen	McLaren	56	1'33"242	336,8
F. Alonso	Renault	45	1'33"536	338,0
G. Fisichella	Renault	54	1'33"563	339,3
C. Klien	Red Bull	43	1'33"727	339,4
R. Schumacher	Toyota	44	1'34"035	325,8
F. Massa	Sauber	43	1'34"094	333,8
M. Webber	Williams	53	1'34"271	335,2
J.P. Montoya	McLaren	15	1'34"501	340,6
A. Pizzonia	Williams	52	1'34"560	336,0
D. Coulthard	Red Bull	54	1'34"585	338,6
J. Villeneuve	Sauber	53	1'34"713	340,1
J. Button	BAR	53	1'34"766	338,3
R. Barrichello	Ferrari	18	1'35"011	336,0
J. Trulli	Toyota	16	1'35"347	328,4
T. Sato	BAR	17	1'35"587	336,2
M. Schumacher	Ferrari	16	1'35"877	342,6
T. Monteiro	Jordan	13	1'36"563	331,6
R. Doornbos	Minardi	54	1'36"894	334,6
C. Albers	Minardi	48	1'37"215	336,0
N. Karthikeyan	Jordan	17	1'37"398	332,2

CHINESE GP

SHANGAI
Length:
5,451 km
Laps: **56**
Distance:
305,066 kms

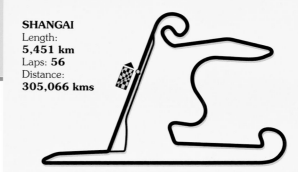

WE ARE THE CHAMPIONS!

This was the chant that the entire world heard on live TV through microphones linked to the team after Alonso crossed the finishing line in Shanghai to give Renault their first ever Constructors' title.

It was a well-deserved title, won against their McLaren rival that had become ultra-competitive towards the end of the season.

The race had almost been won in qualifying when the two Renaults made a lock-out of the front row of the grid. Fisichella then ably shut out Raikkonen after the start and then kept the situation under control, allowing Alonso to build up a sizeable lead in the early laps.

Before the start, there was an incredible incident on the recognition lap. Albers in a Minardi was following Michael Schumacher when he inexplicably accelerated while the Ferrari driver slowed. The Dutchman slammed into and over the Ferrari, wrecking the two cars, which meant that both had to start from the pit-lane in their spare cars.

It was a totally disastrous way to end the season for the Prancing Horse team.

The race boiled down to a battle between Renault and McLaren for the Constructors' title. Any result was possible, with the four drivers fighting for the top 4 places, until Montoya ruined the spectacle by damaging his suspension on a piece of grating thrown up by the powerful Formula 1 cars.

At this point McLaren's hopes of winning were dashed because Alonso was leading and Fisichella third, immediately behind Raikkonen, who had overtaken him during the pit stop.

Not even the entry of the Safety Car for a massive accident involving Karthikeyan's Jordan and a drive-through penalty handed out to Fisichella for holding up Raikkonen when they returned to the pits, which lost the Italian one position, prevented the French Renault team from taking the first-ever Constructors' championship title in their history.

Minardi is to become "Squadra Toro Rosso" (Red Bull Team), written in Italian, but hopefully this is just an error caused by excessive haste to change the name. Minardi have always been a small team in Formula 1 but over the years they have launched several talented young drivers and have always aroused the affection of the entire Formula 1 Circus and the support of the fans. The rapid disappearance of Giancarlo Minardi's team is probably the saddest thing about this year's exciting championship. Thank you Minardi.

Alonso scored his seventh win of the year and Renault took the Constructors' title. The Formula 1 Circus said goodbye to 2005 championship and the Minardi team left its 'mark' as it signed off after 20 years of F1.

	CHAMPIONSHIPS POINTS	AUSTRALIAN GP	MALAYSIAN GP	BAHRAIN GP	SAN MARINO GP	SPANISH GP	MONACO GP	EUROPEAN GP	CANADIAN GP	UNITED STATES GP	FRENCH GP	BRITISH GP	GERMAN GP	HUNGARIAN GP	TURKISH GP	ITALIAN GP	BELGIUM GP	BRAZILIAN GP	JAPANESE GP	CHINA GP	TOTAL POINT
1	F. ALONSO	6	10	10	10	8	5	10	-	rit.	10	8	10	-	8	8	8	6	6	10	133
2	K. RAIKKONEN	1	-	6	-	10	10	-	10	rit.	8	6	-	10	10	5	10	8	10	8	112
3	M. SCHUMACHER	-	2	-	8	-	2	4	8	10	6	3	4	8	-	-	-	5	2	-	62
4	J.P. MONTOYA	3	5	/	/	2	4	2	sq.	rit.	-	10	8	-	6	10	-	10	-	-	60
5	G. FISICHELLA	10	-	-	-	4	-	3	-	rit.	3	5	5	-	5	6	-	4	8	5	58
6	R. SCHUMACHER	-	4	5	-	5	3	-	3	rit.	2	1	3	6	-	3	2	1	1	6	45
7	J. TRULLI	-	8	8	4	6	-	1	-	rit.	4	-	-	5	3	4	-	-	-	-	43
8	R. BARRICHELLO	8	-	-	-	-	1	6	6	8	-	2	-	-	-	-	4	3	-	-	38
9	J. BUTTON	-	-	-	sq.	sq.	sq.	-	-	rit.	5	4	6	4	4	1	6	2	4	1	37
10	M. WEBBER	4	-	3	2	3	6	-	4	rit.	-	-	-	2	-	-	5	-	5	2	36
11	N. HEIDFELD	-	6	-	3	-	8	8	-	rit.	-	-	-	3	-	/	/	/	/	/	28
12	D. COULTHARD	5	3	1	-	1	-	5	2	rit.	-	-	2	-	2	-	-	-	3	-	24
13	F. MASSA	-	-	2	-	-	-	-	5	rit.	-	-	-	-	-	1	-	-	3	-	11
14	J. VILLENEUVE	-	-	-	-	5	-	-	-	rit.	1	-	-	-	-	-	-	3	-	-	9
15	C. KLIEN	2	1	-	/	/	/	/	1	rit.	-	-	-	-	-	-	1	-	4	-	9
16	T. MONTEIRO	-	-	-	-	-	-	-	-	6	-	-	-	-	-	-	-	1	-	-	7
17	A. WURZ	-	-	-	6	/	/	/	/	/	/	/	/	/	/	/	/	/	/	/	6
18	N. KARTHIKEYAN	-	-	-	-	-	-	-	-	5	-	-	-	-	-	-	-	-	-	-	5
19	C. ALBERS	-	-	-	-	-	-	-	-	4	-	-	-	-	-	-	-	-	-	-	4
20	P. DE LA ROSA	/	/	4	/	/	/	/	/	/	/	/	/	/	/	/	/	/	/	/	4
21	P. FRIESACHER	-	-	-	-	-	-	-	-	3	-	-	-	-	-	-	-	-	-	-	3
22	A. PIZZONIA	/	/	/	/	/	/	/	/	/	/	/	/	/	/	2	-	-	-	-	2
23	V. LIUZZI	/	/	/	1	-	-	-	-	/	/	/	/	/	/	/	/	/	/	/	1
24	T. SATO	-	-	-	sq.	sq.	sq.	-	-	rit.	-	-	-	-	-	1	-	-	-	-	1
25	A. DAVIDSON	/	-	-	/	/	/	/	/	/	/	/	/	/	/	/	/	/	/	/	0
26	R. DOORNBOS	/	/	/	/	/	/	/	/	/	/	/	/	/	/	/	/	-	-	-	0

rit.: Retired   **sq.**: Disqualified

2005 World Championship: Drivers & Constructors

Drivers	Australian	Malaysian	Bahrain	San Marino	Spanish	Monaco	European	Canadian	United States	French	British	German	Hungarian	Turkish	Italian	Belgium	Brazilian	Japanese	China	Total Point
F. Alonso	6	10	10	10	8	5	10	-	R	10	8	10	-	8	8	8	6	6	10	133
K. Raikkonen	1	-	6	-	10	10	-	10	R	8	6	-	10	10	5	10	8	10	8	112
M. Schumacher	-	2	-	8	-	2	4	8	10	6	3	4	8	-	-	-	5	2	-	62
J.P. Montoya	3	5	/	/	2	4	2	Sq.	R	-	10	8	-	6	10	-	10	-	-	60
G. Fisichella	10	-	-	4	-	3	-	R	3	5	5	-	5	6	-	4	8	5	58
R. Schumacher	-	4	5	-	5	3	-	3	R	2	1	3	6	-	3	2	1	1	6	45
J. Trulli	-	8	8	4	6	-	1	-	R	4	-	-	5	3	4	-	-	-	-	43
R. Barrichello	8	-	-	-	-	1	6	6	8	-	2	-	-	-	4	3	-	38
J. Button	-	-	-	Sq.	Sq.	Sq.	-	-	R	5	4	6	4	4	1	6	2	4	1	37
M. Webber	4	-	3	2	3	6	-	4	R	-	-	2	-	5	-	5	2	36
N. Heidfeld	-	6	-	3	-	8	8	-	R	-	-	-	3	-	/	/	-	28
D. Coulthard	5	3	1	-	1	-	5	2	R	-	2	-	2	-	-	-	3	-	24
F. Massa	-	-	2	-	-	-	5	R	-	1	-	-	-	3	11
J. Villeneuve	-	-	-	5	-	-	-	R	1	-	-	-	3	-	-	9
C. Klien	2	1	-	-	-	-	-	1	R	-	-	-	1	-	-	4	9
T. Monteiro	-	-	-	-	-	-	-	6	-	-	-	-	1	-	-	7
A. Wurz	/	/	/	6	/	/	/	/	/	/	/	/	/	/	/	/	/	/	6
N. Karthikeyan	-	-	-	-	-	5	-	-	-	-	-	-	-	-	-	5
C. Albers	-	-	-	-	4	-	-	-	-	-	-	-	-	-	-	4
P. De La Rosa	/	4	/	-	-	-	/	/	/	/	/	/	/	/	/	/	/	/	4
P. Friesacher	-	-	-	-	-	-	3	-	-	-	-	-	-	-	-	3
A. Pizzonia	/	/	/	/	/	/	/	/	/	/	/	/	2	-	-	-	2
V. Liuzzi	/	/	1	-	-	-	-	-	-	-	-	-	-	-	-	1
T. Sato	-	-	Sq.	Sq.	Sq.	-	-	R	-	-	1	-	-	1
R. Doornbos	/	/	/	/	/	/	/	/	-	-	-	-	-	-	-	0
A. Davidson	/	/	/	/	/	/	/	/	/	/	/	/	/	/	/	/	/	0

Constructors	Australian	Malaysian	Bahrain	San Marino	Spanish	Monaco	European	Canadian	United States	French	British	German	Hungarian	Turkish	Italian	Belgium	Brazilian	Japanese	China	Total Point
Renault	16	10	10	10	12	5	13	-	R	13	13	15	-	13	14	8	10	14	15	191
McLaren	4	5	10	6	12	14	2	10	R	8	16	8	10	16	15	10	18	10	8	182
Ferrari	8	2	-	8	-	3	10	14	18	6	5	4	8	-	-	4	8	2	-	100
Toyota	-	12	13	4	11	3	1	3	R	6	1	3	11	3	7	2	1	1	6	88
Williams	4	6	3	5	3	14	8	4	R	-	-	5	-	2	5	-	5	2	66
BAR	-	-	Sq.	Sq.	Sq.	-	-	R	5	4	6	5	4	1	6	2	4	1	38
Red Bull	6	4	1	1	1	-	5	3	R	-	2	-	3	-	-	-	3	4	34
Sauber	-	2	5	-	-	5	R	1	-	1	-	-	-	3	-	3	20
Jordan	-	-	-	-	-	-	11	-	-	-	-	1	-	-	12
Minardi	-	-	-	-	-	7	-	-	-	-	-	-	-	7

Drivers	N° GP	N° Pole Position	N° Giri Veloci	N° Ritiri	Australian	Malaysian	Bahrain	San Marino	Spanish	Monaco	European	Canadian	United States	French	British	German	Hungarian	Turkish	Italian	Belgium	Brazilian	Japanese	China
F. Alonso	19	6	2	1	3	1	1	1	2	4	1	-	R	1	2	1	11	2	2	2	3	3	1
K. Raikkonen	19	5	10	1	8	9	3	-	1	1	-	R	2	3	-	1	1	4	1	2	1	2
M. Schumacher	19	1	3	-	-	7	-	2	-	7	5	2	1	3	6	5	2	-	10	-	4	7	-
J.P. Montoya	17	2	1	1	6	4	/	/	7	5	7	Sq.	-	1	-	2	-	3	1	-	1	-
G. Fisichella	19	1	1	1	1	-	-	-	5	12	6	-	6	4	4	9	4	3	-	5	2	4
R. Schumacher	19	1	1	1	12	5	4	9	4	6	-	R	7	8	6	3	12	6	7	8	8	3
J. Trulli	19	1	-	1	9	2	2	5	3	10	8	-	R	5	9	-	4	6	5	-	13	-	15
R. Barrichello	19	-	-	-	2	-	9	-	9	8	3	3	2	9	7	10	10	10	12	5	6	11	12
J. Button	17	1	1	1	11	-	-	Sq.	Sq.	Sq.	10	-	R	4	5	3	5	5	8	3	7	5	8
M. Webber	19	-	-	1	5	-	6	7	6	3	-	5	R	12	11	-	7	-	14	4	-	4	7
N. Heidfeld	14	1	1	-	-	3	-	6	10	2	2	-	R	14	12	11	6	-	-
D. Coulthard	19	-	-	1	4	6	8	11	8	-	4	7	R	10	13	7	-	7	15	-	-	6	9
F. Massa	19	-	-	1	10	10	7	10	-	9	14	4	-	R	10	8	14	-	9	10	11	10	6
J. Villeneuve	19	-	-	1	13	-	11	4	-	11	13	9	R	8	14	15	-	11	11	6	12	12	10
C. Klien	19	-	-	1	7	8	-	-	-	8	-	R	-	15	9	-	8	13	9	9	9	5
T. Monteiro	19	-	-	-	16	12	14	13	12	15	10	3	13	17	13	15	17	18	-	13	11
A. Wurz	1	-	-	-	/	/	/	3	/	/	/	/	/	/	/	/	/	/	/	/	/	/	/
N. Karthikeyan	19	-	-	1	15	11	-	12	13	-	16	-	4	15	-	16	12	14	20	11	15	15	-
C. Albers	19	-	-	-	-	13	13	-	-	14	17	11	5	-	18	13	-	-	19	12	14	16	-
P. De La Rosa	1	-	1	-	-	5	/	/	/	/	/	/	/	/	/	/	/	/	/	/	/	/	/
P. Friesacher	11												6	-	-	-
A. Pizzonia	5												7	-	-	-
V. Liuzzi	4						8	-	-	-
T. Sato	17	-	-	1	-	-	Sq.	Sq.	Sq.	-	-	R	-	-	-	1	-	-
R. Doornbos	8								-	-	-	-	-	-	-
A. Davidson	1				/	/	/	/	/	/	/	/	/	/	/	/	/	/	/	/	/

· R: retired   · Sq.: disqualified

World Champions 1950-2005

N. Farina	(I - Alfa Romeo)	1950		M. Andretti	(USA - Lotus)	1978	Lotus
J.M. Fangio	(RA - Alfa Romeo)	1951		J. Scheckter	(ZA - Ferrari)	1979	Ferrari
A. Ascari	(I - Ferrari)	1952		A. Jones	(AUS - Williams)	1980	Williams
A. Ascari	(I - Ferrari)	1953		N. Piquet	(BR - Brabham)	1981	Williams
J.M. Fangio	(RA - Maserati, Mercedes)	1954		K. Rosberg	(SF - Williams)	1982	Ferrari
J.M. Fangio	(RA - Mercedes)	1955		N. Piquet	(BR - Brabham)	1983	Ferrari
J.M. Fangio	(RA - Ferrari)	1956		N. Lauda	(A - McLaren)	1984	McLaren
J.M. Fangio	(RA - Maserati)	1957		A. Prost	(F - McLaren)	1985	McLaren
M. Hawthorn	(GB - Ferrari)	1958	Vanwall	A. Prost	(F - McLaren)	1986	Williams
J. Brabham	(AUS - Cooper)	1959	Cooper	N. Piquet	(BR - Williams)	1987	Williams
J. Brabham	(AUS - Cooper)	1960	Cooper	A. Senna	(BR - McLaren)	1988	McLaren
P. Hill	(USA - Ferrari)	1961	Ferrari	A. Prost	(F - McLaren)	1989	McLaren
G. Hill	(GB - Brm)	1962	Brm	A. Senna	(BR - McLaren)	1990	McLaren
J. Clark	(GB - Lotus)	1963	Lotus	A. Senna	(BR - McLaren)	1991	McLaren
J. Surtees	(GB - Ferrari)	1964	Ferrari	N. Mansell	(GB - Williams)	1992	Williams
J. Clark	(GB - Lotus)	1965	Lotus	A. Prost	(F - Williams)	1993	Williams
J. Brabham	(AUS - Brabham)	1966	Brabham	M. Schumacher	(D - Benetton)	1994	Williams
D. Hulme	(NZ - Brabham)	1967	Brabham	M. Schumacher	(D - Benetton)	1995	Benetton
G. Hill	(GB - Lotus)	1968	Lotus	D. Hill	(GB - Williams)	1996	Williams
J. Stewart	(GB - Matra)	1969	Matra	J. Villeneuve	(CDN - Williams)	1997	Williams
J. Rindt	(A - Lotus)	1970	Lotus	M. Hakkinen	(FIN - McLaren)	1998	McLaren
J. Stewart	(GB - Tyrrell)	1971	Tyrrell	M. Hakkinen	(FIN - McLaren)	1999	Ferrari
E. Fittipaldi	(BR - Lotus)	1972	Lotus	M. Schumacher	(D - Ferrari)	2000	Ferrari
J. Stewart	(GB - Tyrrell)	1973	Lotus	M. Schumacher	(D - Ferrari)	2001	Ferrari
E. Fittipaldi	(BR - McLaren)	1974	McLaren	M. Schumacher	(D - Ferrari)	2002	Ferrari
N. Lauda	(A - Ferrari)	1975	Ferrari	M. Schumacher	(D - Ferrari)	2003	Ferrari
J. Hunt	(GB - McLaren)	1976	Ferrari	M. Schumacher	(D - Ferrari)	2004	Ferrari
N. Lauda	(A - Ferrari)	1977	Ferrari	F. Alonso	(ESP - Renault)	2005	Renault

2005

Fotografia
Photography
Fotografía
Fotografie

FRITS VAN ELDIK - PAOLO D'ALESSIO - JOHN MARSH - OLIVER RECK

Disegni tecnici
Cutaways
Dibujos Técnicos
Illustraties

PAOLO D'ALESSIO

Realizzazione grafica
Graphic realization
Realización Gráfica
Grafische vormgeving

DIEGO GALBIATI

Traduzioni
Translations
Traducciones
Vertaling

**JULIAN THOMAS &
CENTRO TRADUZIONI IMOLESE**

Stampa
Printing
Impresión
Druck

EDITORIALE LLOYD - TRIESTE (ITALY)

Legatoria
Binding
Encuadernación
Binder

LEGATORIA FRIULIA - MANIAGO-PN (ITALY)

Realizzazione
Editorial production
Realización
Redactie en samenstelling

**© 2005 WORLDWIDE
SEP EDITRICE - CASSINA DE PECCHI
(MILANO - ITALY)
www.sepeditrice.com**

Member of the
World Sportpublisher's Association

Printed in Italy - November 2005

© 2005 SEP Editrice - Cassina de Pecchi (Milano - ITALY)
ISBN 88-87110-57-3

Si ringrazia
AUTOSPRINT
settimanale di automobilismo sportivo leader in Italia,
fonte inesauribile di informazioni e dati statistici ripresi per questo libro.